ARABIC   ASTRONOMY   BA▮▮▮▮▮▮▮▮▮
NISATION   CALCULUS   CA▮  ▮▮▮Y
OMMERCIAL CORRESPONDENCE   ▮▮▮▮▮▮▮▮D
ING   CRICKET   DRAWING   DRESSMAKING   DUTCH   DUTTON
ELECTRICITY IN THE HOUSE   ELOCUTIONIST   EMBROIDERY
ENGLISH RENASCENCE TO THE ROMANTIC REVIVAL   ROMANTIC
VERYDAY FRENCH   TO EXPRESS YOURSELF   FISHING   TO FLY
E BOOK   GARDENING   GAS IN THE HOUSE   GEOGRAPHY OF
NARY   GERMAN GRAMMAR   GERMAN PHRASE BOOK   GOLF
GOOD FARM ACCOUNTING   GOOD FARM CROPS   GOOD FARMING
FARMING   GOOD GRASSLAND   GOOD AND HEALTHY ANIMALS
GOOD POULTRY KEEPING   GOOD SHEEP FARMING   GOOD SOIL
HINDUSTANI   HISTORY: ABRAHAM LINCOLN   ALEXANDER THE
U CONSTANTINE   COOK   CRANMER   ERASMUS   GLADSTONE AND
LTON   PERICLES   PETER THE GREAT   PUSHKIN   RALEIGH   RICHELIEU
DROW Y▮▮▮   ▮EMENT
AN   LETTER
NGIN   ANICS
DERN   · · · · AND HE WILL BE   ORING
ILOSO   HYSICS
UMBI   YET WISER *Proverbs 9.9*   UBLIC
ECKO   USSIAN
ITS N▮   ▮▮▮ AND PURPOSE   SOCCER   SPANISH   SPE▮▮▮   AND
SWA▮   ▮SWEDISH   TEACHING   THINKING   TRIG▮▮▮METRY
BRITI▮H RAILWAYS FOR BOYS   CAMPING FOR BOYS AND GIRLS
OR GIRLS   MODELMAKING FOR BOYS   NEEDLEWORK FOR GIRLS
YS AND GIRLS   SAILING AND SMALL BOATS FOR BOYS AND GIRLS
RK FOR BOYS   ADVERTISING & PUBLICITY   ALGEBRA   AMATEUR
NG   BIOLOGY   BOOK-KEEPING   BRICKWORK   BRINGING UP
RY   CHEMISTRY   CHESS   CHINESE   COMMERCIAL ARITHMETIC
RAVELLING   TO COMPOSE MUSIC   CONSTRUCTIONAL DETAILS
G   DUTCH   DUTTON SPEEDWORDS   ECONOMIC GEOGRAPHY
EMBROIDERY   ENGLISH GRAMMAR   LITERARY APPRECIATION
AL   ROMANTIC REVIVAL   VICTORIAN AGE   CONTEMPORARY
FISHING   TO FLY   FREELANCE WRITING   FRENCH   FRENCH
USE   GEOGRAPHY OF LIVING THINGS   GEOLOGY   GEOMETRY
SE BOOK   GOLF   GOOD CONTROL OF INSECT PESTS   GOOD
ARM CROPS   GOOD FARMING   GOOD FARMING BY MACHINE
GOOD AND HEALTHY ANIMALS   GOOD MARKET GARDENING
GOOD SHEEP FARMING   GOOD SOIL   GOOD ENGLISH   GREEK
RY: ABRAHAM LINCOLN   ALEXANDER THE GREAT   BOLIVAR   BOTHA
ANMER   ERASMUS   GLADSTONE AND LIBERALISM   HENRY V   JOAN OF
T   PUSHKIN   RALEIGH   RICHELIEU   ROBESPIERRE   THOMAS JEFFERSON
OME NURSING   HORSE MANAGEMENT   HOUSEHOLD DOCTOR
RNALISM   LATIN   LAWN TENNIS   LETTER WRITER   MALAY
NENTS   WORKSHOP PRACTICE   MECHANICS   MECHANICAL
MORE GERMAN   MOTHERCRAFT   MOTORING   MOTOR CYCLING
HY   PHYSICAL GEOGRAPHY   PHYSICS   PHYSIOLOGY   PITMAN'S
ESE   PSYCHOLOGY   PUBLIC ADMINISTRATION   PUBLIC SPEAKING

THE TEACH YOURSELF BOOKS
EDITED BY LEONARD CUTTS

TEACH YOURSELF
TO STUDY

TEACH YOURSELF
TO STUDY

By
G. G. NEILL WRIGHT,
M.A., B.ED., D.LITT.

THE ENGLISH UNIVERSITIES PRESS LTD
102 NEWGATE STREET
LONDON, E.C.1

First Printed   1945
This Impression   1960

PRINTED AND BOUND IN ENGLAND
FOR THE ENGLISH UNIVERSITIES PRESS LTD
BY HAZELL WATSON AND VINEY LTD, AYLESBURY

PREFACE

THERE is a saying that every man over forty is either a fool or a doctor. There ought to be a saying that every student is either something of a psychologist or something of a failure, for some understanding of the mind is necessary, if it is to be successfully directed in study. To promote such understanding is the aim of this book.

It should, of course, be studied by the methods recommended in it. That would be a kind of poetic justice, as well as the quickest way to test its usefulness. Unfortunately it would be almost as difficult as lifting oneself by one's own bootstraps. It may, however, be suggested to the reader that he turn first to p. 219 and then, if he choose, give the book a dose of its own medicine. If, for example, he is looking for hints and tips, he may prefer to begin with the later chapters and turn afterwards to the earlier ones for the why and wherefore.

Psychologists study human beings. Other scientists study such things as frogs, fossils, gases, stars, fungi, germs, historical events or economic processes, and it is usually quite easy to tell which is the scientist and which is the frog, fossil or whatever it may be. It is not always so easy to tell which is the psychologist and which is the human being. To avoid mistakes it is, therefore, customary to refer to the latter as the *subject*, and the word is used in this sense when required.

The reader is strongly urged to try upon himself or his friends all the experiments which are suggested in the text. He will learn more about the mind in this way than by merely reading about it.

The author wishes to record his indebtedness to Dr. H. J. Wright for reading his manuscript and making many valuable criticisms and suggestions.

1945   G. G. N. W.

Since first publication in 1945 a few improvements
and additions have been made in successive impressions,
some at the suggestion of readers.   It is hoped that these
may add to the interest and usefulness of the book.

1955   G. G. N. W.

CONTENTS

Part I

LIVING AND LEARNING

Part II

THE GROWTH OF KNOWLEDGE

Part III

THE CONDUCT OF THE MIND

Part IV

THE TOOLS OF STUDY

ACKNOWLEDGMENTS

Acknowledgments are due to the Proprietors of *Punch* for permission to reproduce the drawing on p.116, and to Professor Daniel Starch for the use of the diagram of a learning experiment, on page 157, from *The Journal of Educational Psychology*, 1912, Vol. III, No. 4, page 212.

Part I

LIVING AND LEARNING

CHAPTER I

A CHANGING SOCIETY

Late as it is, I put myself to school,
And feel some comfort not to be a fool.

Beholding the bright countenance of truth in the quiet
and still air of delightful studies.

We are all, as the proverb " Live and learn " implies,
learners in some degree; for, whatever we may be engaged
in, some improvement in skill or understanding comes
unsought with increasing experience. To seek such
improvement deliberately is to become a student,
whether we seek it under the instruction of professional
teachers or by our unaided efforts. We may wish to
qualify ourselves for the practice of a trade or profession,
or to increase our competence at one which we already
follow. We may be concerned with interests which
enrich our leisure, whether they are those of scholarship,
art or science, or hobbies or games of skill. As citizens
of the state, or members of such groups as a church,
trade union, family, or club, we may desire a better
understanding of the social world in which we live and
increased ability to play our part in it.

There are many more students to-day than at any
other period in our history. The social revolution of our
times has provided greater opportunities at the same
time that it has required of us greater technical know-

Note.—The quotations at the head of the chapter are from Pope—*Satires and
Epistles of Horace Imitated*, Ep. I, 1, ll, 47-48 ; John Milton—*Reason of Church
Government*, II, 1, introd.

ledge in all walks of life and imposed upon us more complex duties and responsibilities. New opportunities match new needs.

A peasant or a craftsman in a primitive society learned in childhood and youth the arts practised by the adults of his little community, and in his turn he practised them throughout his life with little change. The great cultures grew slowly until in the sixteenth and seventeenth centuries there began the rapid increase in scientific knowledge and the invention of machines, which continues in our own day. Within our own lifetimes the tractor is taking the place of the horse on the farm, the motor car and the aeroplane compete with the railway, and wireless transmission has made even the telegraph seem old-fashioned. The needs of war and peace have stimulated the invention of new weapons, and new methods of producing and storing food and preventing or treating disease. The new devices so created make it necessary for those who handle them to have new knowledge and new skill. In the words of Professor Whitehead :

> . . . in the past the time-span of important changes was considerably longer than that of a single human life. . . . To-day this time-span is considerably shorter than that of human life, and accordingly our training must prepare individuals to face a novelty of conditions.*

Whether we count ourselves old dogs or young ones, we all have to learn new tricks.

These changes affect us not only as workers but as citizens. Seventy years ago it had become necessary for all members of a modern community to be able to read and write, so necessary that elementary education was made compulsory. This, and the development of

---

*A. N. Whitehead—*Adventures of Ideas,* Pelican Books, p. 94.

the newspaper, made it possible for all citizens to be informed on public affairs. Along with it went the extensions of the franchise which have given to each of us a share in the responsibility for public policy. More recently the radio set in almost every home has made it possible for the Prime Minister at a moment of crisis to address simultaneously all the citizens of a great empire, as a political leader in a small Greek State in ancient times addressed all his fellow citizens gathered together in the place of public assembly. We are all called to take part in the great council of the nation.

Political problems have at the same time become wider in scope. The kind of world we are to live in depends not on British policy alone but on decisions taken in common by all the great nations. Thus, not only are more citizens called upon to take part in shaping public policy, but their decisions affect far larger numbers of men and women and far greater areas of the earth's surface. These more complex problems need wider knowledge if valid solutions are to be reached. Thus we have all become not only members of a community of unexampled size and complexity but members of an international jury participating in the shaping of policies of wider than national significance. The post-war world cannot be a Utopia, but it may well be an improvement on the pre-war world, for we have learned much to which, before the war, we shut our eyes and our minds. The extent to which it will be an improvement depends largely upon ourselves, upon our ability to learn the lessons of our experience, and to see and make use of the opportunities which will be open to us. These opportunities belong for the most part to a larger world than that of our daily life and personal contacts, a world to be known only through the printed word and a disciplined imagination.

The early advocates of universal education sometimes
spoke as if the schools must teach the basic subjects,
reading, writing and counting, to all, and the rest might
be left for each individual to do for himself. We have
long found it necessary to go beyond this in the elementary school, and we now see that some kind of secondary
education is needed for everyone. Nor is this all, for
the need for study does not end with attendance at a
school, or even a technical college or a university. What
such educational institutions provide is not so much an
equipment for life as a groundwork of knowledge, and
some skill with the tools of study, which will enable us
to extend our knowledge in new directions in accordance
with future needs and desires, which cannot be foreseen
with any completeness. In this way only can we have
the adaptability required by a changing society.

For these reasons study is no longer the occupation of
a specialised and segregated few, nor is it confined to
educational institutions. We expect the doctor or the
parson to be a student all his life, to keep himself up to
date so that we, his patients or parishioners, may have
the advantage of new discoveries and new scholarship at
second-hand. There are other fields in which we have
no such professional guides and must keep in touch with
new developments by our own efforts. A century ago
this could be done only by the study of learned books,
written for the learned, and as hard to procure as to read.
To-day it is otherwise. The great originator of knowledge—philosopher, scientist or scholar—may himself
seek a popular audience. If he does not choose to do so,
his ideas may yet reach the public through the medium
of the populariser—the writer who combines an adequate
grasp of what is being done in his own department of
knowledge with a gift for simple exposition. There is
now no important branch of knowledge that cannot be

studied in cheap manuals written by competent scholars, which make learning easy, and such manuals are reaching a wider public every day. Through the journalist and the newspaper more popular accounts of new discoveries and new views reach an even wider public. And our studies need not be confined to the books and newspapers which we can afford to buy, for the Public Libraries will lend us the more advanced and expensive volumes that we want, and the services which they give need only our own increased demands upon them to stimulate their further growth.

A student at one of our older universities works under the direction of a tutor. In this way he learns not only from the printed word but by personal contact with a scholar who has himself made contributions to the subject upon which they are engaged. One of the principal advantages of this method is that he acquires not only a knowledge of his subject but, in less explicit and more subtle ways, a knowledge of how to study it. He is inside the workshop and he sees how the master handles the tools. A Scottish student, or a student at one of the newer English universities does not have this advantage, or does not have it in the same degree. The private student does not have it at all. The result may be much misdirected effort, for there is a technique of study as well as of any other activity.

To study is to set about learning something or other in a deliberate manner, that is, on a definite plan. The solitary student must devise his own plan. He is both teacher and pupil and so he has a double responsibility, the responsibility for directing his own efforts as well as making them. As teacher he must decide what he is to read, or what and when and for how long he is to practise, and the like. His success will depend largely upon such decisions, for in study as in other matters a relatively small amount of effort effectively directed will accomplish more than much greater effort misdirected.

Such misdirection is common. Study is too often thought of as a process of passive absorption : the student tries to soak up knowledge as a piece of blotting-paper soaks up ink. He sits in front of the printed page until its words are impressed upon his mind as permanently as on the paper. Trying to turn himself into a recording apparatus like a gramophone disc or a photographic plate, he takes for his ideal a mind which is :

Wax to receive and marble to retain.*

This is a false ideal, for mind and body are not designed to work in that way. They are not an apparatus for recording but an apparatus for doing ; and learning, to be effective, must be an active, not a passive, process.

It is not difficult to see how this misapprehension has arisen. It is easier to test what a student can remember than what he can do. Examinations thus become largely tests of memory and so teachers and pupils, more interested in passing the examinations than in mastering the subjects they are studying, put an undue emphasis on memory work. It is also the line of least resistance for the teacher. Nothing is easier than to set the pupil to " get up " something, and then set a test upon it—and an imposition on the top of that, if the test is not passed satisfactorily. The pupil, faced with responsibilities which belong properly to the teacher and not knowing any better, in too many cases resorts to mere memorising ; and, unfortunately, he too often succeeds by this means in meeting the demands of the teacher and the examiner. Such a system is neither teaching nor learning, but a travesty of both. To have a good memory is to have a good and useful servant, but one

---

* Byron—*Beppo*, 34.

whose services, indispensible in their place, are not of universal application.

According to Aristotle, we learn how to do things by doing the things we want to be able to do.* We do not make any mistake about this in the case of skill at a craft or a game. No one supposes that he has learned to use a lathe or to bowl googlies, because he has got by heart a page or two of the book of instructions. Skill at such things can be acquired only by practice—by doing the things we want to be able to do. The book of instructions has its uses. From a book or from a teacher we may gather some hints as to how we may best set about doing the thing we want to be able to do, but the doing of it is the essential thing.

The student's first problem is therefore : *What do I want to be able to do ?* and his second, *How do I set about doing it ?* He is seeking to acquire a new power of managing a tool or a club or a machine, or a new power of using his mind to observe or imagine or appreciate or understand or interpret or invent or reason or judge or recognise or predict, or a new power of guiding or advising or inspiring or directing or organising or leading others. In any of these cases memory may have a part to play, but it is a subordinate one. We have to remember the golf teacher's instructions to keep the head steady and take the club back slowly, we have to remember the factors of $a^2 - b^2$, or the importance of putting the clutch out before pulling at the gear lever, or that " Green to green or red to red, Means perfect safety, go ahead." But the work of the memory is merely incidental. The emphasis is in every case on the power to be acquired. The champion golfer is not engaged in remembering to keep his head steady ; his nerves and muscles do that

---

* " For the things we have to learn before we can do them, we learn by doing them. *e.g.* men become builders by building and lyre-players by playing the lyre . . ."—*Aristotle, Selections*, ed. W. D. Ross, p. 230.

for him while he is engaged in doing what he wants to do to the ball. The mathematician "sees" the difference of two squares as the product of their sum and difference as soon as he sees the printed symbols. The motor driver and the navigator take the appropriate action without stopping to think.

The same is true of other studies, though it may not be so evident that we can learn to think only by thinking, or that to read a book in any useful sense our minds must be active in much the same way that the author's was in writing it. To work at history or mathematics, at a foreign language or a branch of engineering, is to seek new powers of doing something, not this time with the limbs and fingers, but with the mind. What is sought is a new power of thinking or understanding, a command of new instruments, mental ones this time, such as the multiplication table, the terms and conceptions of a science, or the vocabulary and idiom of a foreign language. It is significant that we speak of *mastering* such material, mastering it as we master a horse or a motor bicycle, gaining control over it, so that it answers our desires and serves our purposes, becoming a part of ourselves almost like an arm or a leg.

In studying, therefore, we should not sit and look at what is before us. We should on all occasions do something with it. Practise it. Test it. Apply it. Tell it to someone else. Criticise it. Argue against it. Deduce its consequences. Examine the evidence for it. Summarise it. Expand it. Seek for instances which exemplify it. At the very worst copy it out. In this way our mental powers are set to work upon it and it becomes to be incorporated with them. These powers are thus extended, for the mind is a living and growing thing.

For this reason the nature of study is much better indicated by the old-fashioned phrase which speaks of the student as " cultivating his mind " than by the metaphor of wax and marble. The growth of the mind takes place in accordance with its own laws. We do not expect to cultivate a garden successfully without some knowledge of gardening, some knowledge of times and seasons and the parts played by soil and temperature, sun and rain ; for plants are living things and must grow according to the laws of their own nature. The cultivation of the mind is similarly aided by some knowledge of the laws of mental growth.

CHAPTER II

OUR SERVANT, THE BODY

Whether priority be to Matter or Mind
(A fit debate for prizefighter and don). . . .

What is't to live, if not to pull the strings
Of thought that pull those grosser strings whereby
We pull our limbs to pull material things
Into such shape as in our thoughts doth lie ?

" I teach myself. . . ." What is the self that is
submitted to this process of instruction, and what do
" I " know about it ?

Each of us has a considerable knowledge of himself
acquired during an acquaintance which has lasted as
long as his conscious life. W. S. Gilbert's Lord Chancellor,
at a crisis in his affairs, when as a suitor he had applied
to himself for the hand of his own ward in marriage, and
was of a mind to deal sternly with this presumption,
reminded himself that he had known himself for a
considerable time, that he had watched his professional
advancement with considerable interest, and that he
yielded to no one in admiration for his private and
professional virtues. This incident is a witty application
of the truth that there is for all of us a division, or at
least a distinction, between " myself " as known to me
and the " I " which enjoys this acquaintance.

We constantly use this knowledge in regulating our
affairs. In arranging a meal or a holiday we use our
knowledge of restaurants or foods, of roads and railways,
prices and climates, opportunities for fishing or climbing ;
but we also use, less deliberately, our knowledge of our

Note.—The quotations at the head of the chapter are from : R. M Hewitt—
Sonnets for Helen, 1927, " Eva " ; *The Note-Books of Samuel Butler*, ed. H. Festing
Jones, 1918, p. 396.

tastes, our habits and our interests. In this way our self-knowledge enters into most of our deliberations and decisions.

There is therefore no new principle involved in seeking to understand how one's body and mind play their parts in learning something new. A man knows that he needs three or four meals a day, that if he gets insufficient sleep he becomes irritable and unfit for his work, that it is better to avoid certain foods or too much tobacco, that he has certain likes and dislikes, or certain faults of temper against which he must be on his guard, and he regulates his life accordingly. It is like understanding a piece of machinery that one is operating and so being able to get the best out of it. It is only commonsense to do the same with one's studies.

The machine the student is operating is his own mind and body. These are so closely connected that both have parts to play in all that we do. Both are possessed of unexpected powers. Both are servants whose co-operation must be secured. Together they constitute the most delicate and complex, as well as the most powerful kind of apparatus in the world.

The body is in some ways the easier of the two to understand. It is in some respects like a machine, and we are familiar with machines, and know how they are made and how to manage them. The body, like a machine, will do much for us without our active intervention. Thus our breathing is so regulated as to keep the proportion of carbon dioxide in our lungs constant within a variation of one-fifth of one per cent. Indoors and outdoors, summer and winter, the temperature of the body is kept close to 98.4° F., and if it rises as far as to 99° we feel that something is wrong. The pupil of the eye opens and closes with every change in the intensity of the light, so that at all times the amount of light admitted by it is such as to allow the clearest and most comfortable vision possible. Our muscles answer to our desires. When the expert craftsman picks up a tool, or the expert player a club or a ball, he finds his limbs and fingers ready to carry out the wanted movement.

A machine needs supervision, and so in different degrees do the acts which we delegate to the body. Breathing will look after itself as a rule, but in swimming with the overhand stroke that brings the head under water we must so regulate it that we breathe in when the head emerges ; and on the alarm of gas we must consciously hold our breath as we pull on the respirator. Sometimes when the supervision fails the results are amusing. An old gentlemen goes upstairs to change for dinner. Wrapt in thought he begins to undress, but at the vital moment, when he should get into his dress-shirt, he picks up his pyjamas and proceeds to go to bed. Someone sets out for the golf course, and finds that he has taken the wrong turning and is well on the way to his place of business. Mr. X, during a period of overwork, reaches his office door, sees the indicator set to " Mr. X— OUT," and turns away in annoyance with the thought, " I must come back to-morrow." A teacher of mathematics, meditating upon some piece of algebra and fingering a piece of chalk in his pocket, as he walks along the street, finds himself facing the black, smooth back of a cab and proceeds to work out his problem upon it, walking after it as it moves off, and wondering dimly what new kind of mobile blackboard has been inflicted upon him. Such anecdotes are all of the same type as the classical story of the astronomer who fell down a well while looking at the stars.

Such incidents—and they happen to all of us—show that our acts are not all conscious and deliberate. As a rule it is only when something goes wrong that this fact is brought to our notice. But the astonishing thing—when we do notice and reflect upon it—is that so great a part of our conduct is carried out for us without our deliberate guidance. The surprising thing is not that mistakes happen but that they happen so seldom. By far the greater part of our actions take place with little thought. It takes a conscious resolution to get out of bed, but once the feet are on the floor the successive acts of dressing go on more or less automatically. It may be difficult to make up one's mind to go and shave, or dig the garden, or put on a coat and go for a walk, but once the train of action is initiated it seems to go on more or less by itself.

This may be illustrated by a simple experiment. Let the reader write the following sentence once or twice with pen or pencil to make himself familiar with it :

" It is, Kit, isn't it ? " said Tit.

Let him now write it again, but this time without lifting the pen between the words, without capital letters, without quotation marks, commas, question mark or period, and without dotting the i's or crossing the t's.

It may at first appear that the second task should be the easier—since there is so much less to be done. The reader has no doubt found that the contrary is the case. At the appropriate moment there is a strong impulse to insert each of the marks that is to be omitted, and a strong effort of attention is required in order to control these impulses. Long ago we learned to write. Each movement was at first deliberate : there was a conscious decision to make each stroke. As a result of practice these movements became habits—actions which we could perform with little attention to them. Now when we try to vary these actions a little we find how independent they are of our conscious direction. The movements which we do not want *interfere* with those which we want.

How are such habitual actions performed ? The actual movements are brought about by our muscles. What initiates and guides their movements ? The simplest answer to this question is, the nervous system— the brain, the spinal cord and the nerves which run from them to every part of the body. Every muscular movement is set going by a nervous impulse, which has travelled to the muscle from some centre in the brain or the spinal cord, through the nerve which connects these two parts. The part played by these nerves is clearly proved by cases in which a nerve has been severed. Control over the muscles to which the severed nerve runs is lost, until the nerve grows together again.

What happens at the centre is less well understood. Here it is enough to say that such centres seem to be the parts of the body most closely connected with the mind, and that it is through them that we control our bodies. When we perform a conscious and deliberate action, we seem to begin by " making up our minds " to do it. This purely mental act seems to be accompanied or followed by some action of the nervous system, which leads to the passage of a nervous impulse to the appropriate muscles, and their movement. When we perform an action without such conscious deliberation, it must be initiated, either in some part of the mind of which we are not normally aware, or in the nervous system itself. We may therefore provisionally think of the nervous system as the machine—or the good servant—which under our personal, but intermittent, supervision, conducts for us the business of living.

This means that we must think of the nervous system as the good servant that masters on our behalf the things we wish to learn : or, putting it another way, when the student, teaching himself, is at once teacher and pupil, he is asking his nervous system to acquire new powers to be used on his behalf as occasion for them arises.

There are two sides to the connection between mind and body. On the one hand it is through bodily organs, the eyes, the ears, the tongue, the nose and the skin (which is sensitive to heat, cold, touch and pain), that we are aware of the world around us. On the other hand it is through the body that we speak and act and so produce effects upon persons and things in the world around us. All our knowledge of the world, our knowledge of our friends, of human speech, of the arts and sciences, has come to us through the senses. Without sense organs our minds would be shut up in silence and darkness. Without control over our muscles we should be impotent spectators of our surroundings.

The plan on which the nervous system is arranged is similarly two-sided. It may be described as a system of connections between *sense organs* and *organs of response*. Nervous impulses always travel in this one direction, that is to say, from sense organ to muscle or gland. Thus it is not unlike a telephone system in which there is only one-way traffic. But nervous impulses are never carried direct from a sense organ to a muscle or a gland : the route is always through a *nerve centre* in the brain or the spinal cord ; and there are always at least two nerves involved in such a connection, one to carry the impulse inward from the sense organ and one to carry it outward to the muscle or gland which is to make the required response. Nerves of the first kind are called *sensory nerves :* those of the second kind are called *motor nerves,* since it is their function to bring about movement.

Examples of this simple arrangement are to be found in the bodily responses called *reflexes*. One of these, the *patellar reflex* or *knee jerk*, is illustrated in Fig. 1. The

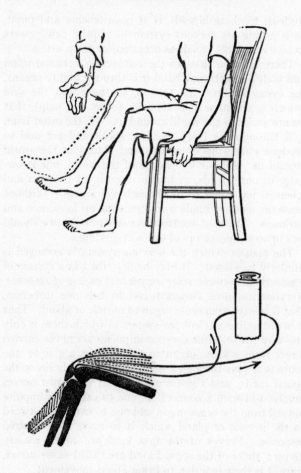

FIG. 1.

Reflex action : the knee jerk. The arrows show the direction in which the nervous impulse passes through the sensory nerve to the spinal cord and through the motor nerve to the muscle.

reader can easily test it for himself.   If one leg be crossed over the other, as shown, and the front of the leg tapped just below the knee-cap (patella), it will be found that the foot kicks up—perhaps much to the surprise of the subject of the experiment.   The response will be repeated as often as the tap is administered.   The explanation is that the tap causes a nervous impulse to travel up the sensory nerve, shown in the second drawing, to a centre in the spinal cord.   There the sensory nerve connects with a motor one through which the nervous impulse passes into the muscle which, by its contraction, pulls up the leg.

Many of our simpler responses are brought about in this way.   Thus, if the fingers inadvertently touch something hot, nerve-endings in the skin are stimulated so that nervous impulses flow up the arm through sensory nerves, which at the centre connect with motor nerves running to the muscles which withdraw the hand from the painful contact.   When we peel onions, the vapour rising from the onions causes the tear glands to be more active and there is a flow of tears.   When the light which enters the eye, and falls upon the sensitive nerve-endings which cover the retina or back wall of the eye, is too bright, the pupil of the eye is contracted so as to admit less, and if it is not bright enough for clear vision the pupil is more widely opened to admit more.   If phlegm obstructs the breathing passages we cough.   In each case there is such an apparatus of sensory and motor nerves as we have described in the case of the knee-jerk.   In each case they are brought into action by some outside event which we call the *stimulus;* and in each case their activity results in a movement of a muscle or some change in the secretion of a gland, which we call the *response.*

Muscles and glands are the only two kinds of organs

of response, and it may therefore be said that there are only two things that human beings can do—move and secrete. Thus, to speak is to produce sounds by movements of the breathing muscles and the muscles of the larynx, tongue and lips. To eat is to make movements of the jaws, tongue and throat, and to digest is to make movements, involuntary this time, of the stomach and intestines, while secreting the digestive juices needed to prepare the food in these organs for assimilation. To look at human action in this way is to take a very abstract view of it, for what we have to say is no doubt of much greater importance than the movements of the speech organs regarded by themselves ; but, however valuable our thoughts or noble our purposes, we cannot express them in speech or action except through the working of nerves, muscles and glands.

Muscles bring about movement. Every muscle consists of a large number of elongated cells laid side by side, which have the power of becoming shorter and thicker when the nervous impulse reaches them. As each component cell shortens and thickens, the muscle contracts, and so it pulls upon the bone or other structure to which it is attached and causes it to move. All the movements of the body are brought about in this way. Thus, if the reader will extend his right arm, grasp the upper arm between the finger and thumb of the left hand, and then raise the forearm by bending the arm at the elbow, he will feel the muscle under his grasp grow thicker and more tense as the movement is made. Muscles which can be moved at will like this are called *voluntary muscles*. There are other muscles, which, like those of the heart or the intestines, are not under voluntary control, and these are called *involuntary muscles*. Their movements, like those of the voluntary muscles, are caused by nervous impulses flowing into them through motor nerves, but in this case it happens without our knowledge or will.

Glands secrete chemical substances necessary for the economy of the body. It is a case of every man his own chemist's shop. Familiar examples are the *tear glands*, which secrete a saline liquid which washes the eye-ball, and flows more freely when grit or a fly gets in the eye and has to be washed out ; the *salivary glands* under the tongue which produce *saliva* in sufficient quantity to keep the lining of the mouth moist, and in greater quantity when food is being masticated in order to prepare it for digestion ; the *liver* which secrets bile and has several other functions ; the *sweat glands* which play the double part of excreting impurities and of helping to regulate the temperature of the body by moistening its surface in order to cool it by evaporation ; the *sebaceous glands*, also just under the skin, which produce a lubricant to keep the hairs and the skin soft. All these have *ducts*, that is to say, tubes, through which their secretions flow to the places where they are needed. We have in addition *ductless glands*, which secrete small quantities of highly important chemical substances called *hormones*, which are passed into the blood-stream and reach all parts of the body in that way. The activity of the glands, like that of the muscles, is controlled through motor nerves, but this activity, like that of the involuntary muscles, is not under the control of the will.

Our movements and our secretions are *responses*, that is to say, answers, to the stimuli received by our sense organs. Thus it grows colder and we draw nearer the fire. It gets darker and we hold the book higher in order to catch the light from the window, or we switch on the light. Our stomachs become empty, and we seek a meal. Some phlegm gathers in the breathing passages, and we cough to dislodge it. In some of these cases the stimuli are outside the body, in others within it, but the principle is the same. In all of them it is clearly important that the response made should be the appropriate one How is the appropriate response selected ?

The response made depends upon which set of motor nerves the incoming nervous impulses are directed into. It may be doubted whether there is any action so simple that it can be brought about by a single sensory and a single motor nerve. C. S. Sherrington calls this conception " a convenient though improbable abstraction." Even in the case of the knee-jerk a number of sensory nerves must be stimulated and a number of motor nerves must be involved in bringing about the response. In addition there are nerves of a third kind, which intervene between sensory nerves and motor nerves. These are called *connecting nerves*. The response which follows a stimulus depends upon the way in which these connecting nerves are arranged. They may be compared to the exchange in a telephone system, since they do very much the same work. They make up a large part of the bulk of the brain and the spinal cord, and they afford a variety of paths by which an incoming nervous impulse may find its way to an outgoing nerve. It is therefore within these organs that the outgoing path is determined, and that path determines what muscles or glands will be affected and what kind of action will follow.

Thus the whole apparatus of the body—sense organs, nervous system and organs of response—is an apparatus designed for action. This is why learning is an active and not a passive process, although outwardly the learner, listening to a lecture or studying a book, may appear to be merely passive or receptive. We shall see by and by how deceptive this appearance is, if any useful learning is taking place.

Every action which we can perform must be

represented in the nervous system by some piece of nervous apparatus, a set of connecting nerves arranged upon such a plan that they can bring about the movements of which that action consists. If *A* can perform with ease an action of which *B* is incapable—let us say, riding a bicycle or eating boiled rice with chop-sticks—then *A*'s nervous system must contain a set of connecting nerves organised for that purpose which *B*'s nervous system lacks.

It follows that learning a new action, whether it be eating with chop-sticks or solving quadratic equations or speaking Russian, means establishing a new set of connecting nerves which will be called into activity by a new kind of stimulation, and which will in turn arouse in the muscles a new combination of movements. Someone says, " Hullo, how are you ? " and this succession of sounds calls out the reply, " Fine, thanks. How are you ? " To learn another language is to be aroused on a similar occasion by a different pattern of speech sounds, and to make a different succession of sounds in reply, while apprehending and seeking to convey the same meaning. Learning is thus a matter of modifying existing nervous apparatus, so that it may be aroused by new kinds of stimulation, or so that familiar kinds of stimulation may lead to new kinds of response, or so that new connections may be made between familiar kinds of stimulation and responses we are already capable of making.

Whether the mind or soul has any existence or power of learning apart from the body, no one is in a position to say, though opposite views on this question are commonly maintained with a dogmatism which is unsupported by anything that can be called decisive evidence. If the mind or soul has no separate existence, the importance of the nervous system in learning is beyond question. If it has a separate existence, then, so far as our knowledge goes, it can speak only through bodily speech organs and guide a pen, or any other tool, only through the medium of the hand and the fingers, and it can control these organs only through motor nerves. Whatever its potentialities, it can realise them as practical abilities only through the organisation of nervous connections corresponding to the patterns of bodily movement which are needed.

CHAPTER III

NATURAL GROWTH

"Do you know who made you?" "Nobody as I knows on," said the child. . . . "I 'spect I growed."

The apple tree never asks the beech how he shall grow; nor the lion, the horse, how he shall take his prey.

The nervous system is extremely complex. There are some 3,000,000,000 separate connections in the *cortex* (the outer layer of the upper brain) alone. The separate parts are therefore very small. A nerve may be as much as three feet in length—for example, the sensory nerves which run from the tips of the toes to the lower part of the spinal cord—but it is no more than 1/4,000 of an inch in diameter. Moreover, every nerve, although so small, has a complicated structure. Because the nervous system is so complex and because its parts are so minute, the exploration of it (mainly with the help of the microscope) can reveal its general plan but not the details of its working. Our knowledge of the way it works comes largely by inference from observations of a different kind—we can apply different kinds of stimulation to human beings and animals, study the responses made to each kind of stimulation, and infer what kind of connections must exist in the nervous system to bring about these responses.

Looked at in this way the human being may be compared to a mechanical doll. You press some point on the surface of the doll and it makes a sound resembling "ma-ma." You press another point and it makes a sound resembling "da-da." You pull a string and it

Note.—The quotations at the head of the chapter are from: Harriet Beecher Stowe—*Uncle Tom's Cabin*, Chapt. 20; Wm. Blake—*Proverbs of Hell*, ed. G. Keynes, 1927.

raises its arms. You lay it on its back and it closes its eyes. From a series of such experiments you can infer that the doll contains certain pieces of apparatus, each set in motion by a certain kind of pressure, pull or position (stimulation), and each producing a certain kind of result (response).

If we wished to make the mechanical doll answer to new kinds of stimulation or make a new kind of response, we should have to put some new piece of apparatus into it, just as we make a bicycle or a wireless set more versatile by adding a three-speed gear to the one or putting another valve and some more wiring into the other. We cannot insert new gadgets into the nervous system. How, then, do we acquire new pieces of nervous apparatus? The answer is suggested by another question: How did we get those we have already? By growing them.

Of the thousands of millions of nervous connections which we possess, by far the larger number have come into existence without our taking any trouble in the matter. They have come by processes of natural growth, mainly before birth and in infancy and childhood. When we set out to learn something, we are setting out to stimulate the growth of new nervous connections. We are quite literally " cultivating " our nervous systems in the same sense that we cultivate turnips or carrots, by supplying them with the conditions that will encourage the growth of roots of the size and shape that we desire. To understand what this involves, we must first look at what natural growth has done for us without our taking any pains in the matter.

A new-born baby can breathe and cough or sneeze, and very soon it will suck. These highly complex responses cannot have been learned by practising them, since before birth there was neither opportunity nor need. At birth there is need. Without them the child must suffocate or starve. He is, therefore, born with the nervous apparatus which operates them ready to do its work.

These responses are apt to be taken for granted. We have always been able to perform them with ease and so we think of them as easy. Yet they are in fact highly complex.

Consider the act of sucking. It is necessary first to make an air-tight joint with the lips. This in itself is a delicate and complex muscular movement. Next, it is necessary to reduce the air-pressure in the mouth cavity so that the milk will spurt into it. The reader may find it interesting to find out by experiment exactly what movements of lips, tongue, cheeks and soft palate he makes in the act of sucking, and to note that he may make these movements with complete efficiency without knowing at all accurately what they are. Thirdly, the milk must be collected in the mouth in such a way that it does not run back into the breathing passages and cause choking. Fourthly, when enough has been collected, it must be tipped back into the throat so that it may be swallowed. Swallowing is itself a complex muscular movement—and one which some adults find difficult, when some unusual object, such as a pill or a tablet has to be dealt with. Lastly, all these movements must be made in the proper sequence and rhythm. If, instead of being born able to suck, we had to learn, as we have to learn a golf swing, we might find it as difficult and make as poor a job of it.

The nervous connections on which such movements depend have come into existence in the same way as the other organs of the body. During the period before birth the body is formed by processes of the same kind as we can observe in the growth of a plant from a seed. In either case it begins with a single fertilized cell of minute size, which divides into two cells, each of which divides again, until by the continuation of this process many million cells have been formed. These cells vary in shape and character according to the part they are to play in the bodily economy. Some are muscle cells. Some are liver cells, secreting bile. Some form the skin, some the linings of the mouth and the other body cavities. Each organ of the body consists of cells of a particular type according to the work it has to do. At the same time the cells in each are arranged on a suitable plan, so that they may do their work effectively. Muscle cells extend side by side, so that when they contract they all exercise a pull in the same direction. Liver cells are arranged round the ducts through which their secretions are to flow.

A nerve cell originates in the same way as the other cells of the body—by division and growth and redivision. The plan upon which the nerve cells are arranged is in the first instance a result of natural growth, just as in the case of the other bodily organs. Thus, the fact that the new-born child is able to breathe, suck, swallow, digest, excrete, cough, sneeze, cry and move his arms and legs means that the nervous apparatus upon which each of these movements depends has been formed before birth by this process of natural growth and is complete and in working order.

The movements the infant is capable of are strictly limited in number. Thus he cannot stand, walk, speak, reach out to grasp something he sees in front of him or follow a moving object with his eyes. The nervous apparatus for these movements is not yet in working order. Microscopic study of the nervous system reveals two facts of interest here. First, all the nerve cells which the child will ever have are believed to be already present at birth. Secondly, a large proportion of them are not fully formed and therefore are not yet ready to work. If you go into a house which has just been completed by the builders you may find that all the electric wiring is in place, but that the wires are not yet connected up to the switches or to the main. It is useless to try to get a light by pressing a switch for no current can pass. Similarly, the nervous apparatus for the acts of standing, walking, speaking and so on already exists in the infant's body but in an immature or incomplete state. As the child grows older, this apparatus matures and we can observe the appearance of new movements. They appear in a regular order. The process of growth which formed the nervous system before birth is continuing, and it is continuing on a regular plan, just as the growth of a plant (which we can observe more easily) follows a regular plan :

. . . first the blade, then the ear, after that the full corn in the ear.

We are familiar with some such processes of natural growth in our own bodies. Thus, the body as a whole grows steadily bigger and stronger in normal infancy, childhood and adolescence. There is also an alteration in its proportions. At birth the head is about one-quarter of the whole length of the body, at two years of age it is about three-sixteenths, in the adult about one-eighth. The infant's arms and shoulders are disproportionately large, its legs are puny. More rapid growth in height alternates with more rapid growth in girth. The programme of growth differs in the two sexes. Although boys are on the average taller than girls, the girls catch up on the boys between the ages of ten and eleven years and pass them, to be caught and passed again between fifteen and sixteen, so that the average height of men is greater than that of women. Another familiar example of natural growth is the development of the teeth. First come the eight incisors or front teeth, next the four canines or eye-teeth and, by the end of the second year, the four molars or back teeth, twenty teeth in all. These are temporary teeth. About the age of six the first permanent teeth appear, four new molars in the now longer jaw. The temporary teeth become loose as their roots are absorbed, and they fall out to make way for the permanent teeth which are growing underneath them and presently replace them, a process which continues during later childhood and adolescence. These facts are set out as a familiar illustration of a pre-determined programme of growth, because its stages are easily observed and so we can see that a plan is followed which, in its general lines, is the same for everyone, though there may be in individual cases retardations or accelerations and other minor variations. For instance, some persons never cut the last set of molars, the wisdom teeth, at all, and in others they appear belatedly, sometimes as late as the forty-fifth year of life.

The study of the child's behaviour shows a similar predetermined programme of development. The infant does not stand or walk at birth. For this there are three reasons. Firstly, its legs are not strong enough to support its weight. Secondly, the nerves which control the muscles of the legs and trunk in standing and walking, so as to support the weight of the body and balance it on the narrow base afforded by the two feet, are still immature. Thirdly, the infant has no interest in these acts and no desire to perform them. In the course of the first fifteen months of life, the legs grow longer and straighter, the bones and muscles grow stronger. At the same time the nerves controlling these muscles are being linked up with the sense organs which enable us to keep our balance. Thirdly, the child shows an increasing interest in locomotion. He enjoys being carried from place to place. He struggles across the floor on all fours, gaining increasing skill in this mode of locomotion. He tries to get on his feet, pulling himself up by the furniture. So strong are his impulses to do this that he cannot be prevented from attempting it. He moves about clumsily, holding on to chairs and tables. Then, with the encouragement of his parents, he takes a few steps and falls down, and tries again, until he is able to move about in an ungainly and uncertain fashion, placing his feet somewhat widely to avoid falling to left or right and using his arms to help his balance. Thus, becoming able to walk involves bodily growth, which is visible to us, growth of the nervous system, which we can infer from the child's behaviour, and growth which we at once think of as mental growth, the appearance of new interests, new impulses and desires, expressed in the visible striving to do new things. No doubt this also is paralleled in the nervous system by the maturing of further nervous organisation.

We speak of the child " learning to walk." It is doubtful how far learning enters into the process, but it probably plays a part in the later stages. That this part is small is proved by observations of children who, on account of some accident or ailment, have been prevented from attempting to walk until a little later than the usual age. Such children pass more rapidly through the preliminary stages, taking days to " learn " what the normal child takes weeks to acquire at an earlier age. If walking were the result of true learning, we should expect such a child to take just about as long as a younger healthy one.

Nevertheless, it seems probable that practice is necessary to complete the process and that the example of others, parental encouragement and stumbling about, falling and trying again, are the means by which success is finally achieved. It is worth noting that there is evidence that children carried off and brought up by wolves move about on all fours as if their powers of natural growth were not enough to make them assume the upright position without human example.*

The child's toddle is not the end of the matter. He becomes more steady on his feet and ceases to stagger about like a drunken man. He begins to trot and finally to run. The nervous apparatus is becoming more efficient, and practice seems to play an important part in this improvement. By and by he learns to balance himself not only on his feet but on a scooter, and then on a bicycle. There can be no doubt that that these skills are the result of learning and not of natural growth. In special cases still higher degrees of skill may be attained. The tight-rope walker may balance himself on a swaying cable above Niagara, or the sailor boy may gain such a nice control that he can stand upright on the top of the mast of his ship as it sails steadily with a favourable breeze. In these and in all other learned activities it is difficult or impossible to draw a line between what comes by natural growth and what is learned.

In all cases of learning a piece of bodily skill, such as skill at a game or with a tool or a weapon, there is a similar combination of some movement already possessed and something further which is gained by learning. The learner begins with the nearest thing he has in his repertoire of bodily movements. His attempts are therefore clumsy and not very well adapted to his new purpose. With practice they become defter and more efficient. What does this mean in terms of nervous machinery ? It means that the learner begins by using

---

*A. Gesell—*Wolf Child and Human Child*, 1941.

the piece of nervous apparatus most nearly suited to his purpose, and this becomes modified, until it is capable of performing the new movement easily and more accurately. Learning is thus the continuation of neural growth in new directions determined by what the learner sets out to do. This principle applies equally to increase in knowledge or understanding. Just as new skill grows out of old skill, so new knowledge grows out of what is already known.

The new growth is set going as a result of the learner's *interest*, his desire for mastery over the new accomplishment. Its direction is guided by the success or failure of his attempts. If there were no attempts there would be no new neural growth, that is there would be no learning, for there would be no successes and failures to guide it. You learn to ride a bicycle by sometimes falling off and sometimes sticking on, until at last your nervous apparatus makes for you every time the movements which enable you to stick on. Similarly, there would be no improvement if there were no desire to master the new accomplishment. The falling off would not become a less frequent occurrence if there were not a strong desire to stick on.

CHAPTER IV

HAPPY MOMENTS

But it needs happy moments for this skill.

The deep well of unconscious cerebration.

We are all familiar with two different situations in which we may find ourselves when trying to learn something. In the first we feel entirely at a loss. Our fingers are all thumbs. The pen or the brush, the bat or the ball, the fingers or the keys of the typewriter seem possessed of wills of their own. The words we read will not give up their meaning. The figures refuse to be added. In situations of the second kind such difficulties suddenly disappear. Our muscles suddenly get the knack of the new movement, or a sudden and joyous illumination breaks upon the mind ; what was obscure is suddenly clear and everything fits together into an intelligible whole. The art of learning is largely the art of cultivating such happy moments. How may this be done ? How, when such momentary success has been achieved, may it be turned into a permanent accomplishment ? Let us consider these questions first in relation to learning new kinds of skill.

We must first note that it is never possible to make an entirely new movement. We are limited to the repertoire of moments provided by our present systems of motor nerves. What we can do is to isolate any one of these movements and make it by itself, instead of as a part of the pattern of movements in which it normally occurs. We can then combine it with other movements similarly

Note.—The quotations at the head of the chapter are from : Matthew Arnold— *The Scholar-Gipsy:* Henry James—*The American.*

isolated. Thus the reader has probably in moments of vexation or doubt found himself beating the devil's tattoo with his fingers on the table-top or on the arm of his chair. He can make any one of these finger movements deliberately. In learning to play the piano we take advantage of this, striking this key and then that in the required order, with careful attention to the degree of force exerted and the interval of time between one note and the next. We " practise " these movements— that is to say, we repeat them again and again—until less and less attention is needed, and finally they can be performed accurately without any such oversight. The separate finger movements have now been combined in a new way, and it is only necessary to think of this exercise or that scale and our nerves and fingers are ready to play it for us. We have taught our servant, the nervous system, a new accomplishment which it can now carry out for us at need.

Practice of this kind—repetition of movements in learning to write or to dance, to handle a rifle or use a bayonet, repetition of words or numbers, as in so much school work—is commonly spoken of as " drill." Just as the drill sergeant on the barrack square or the teacher in front of the blackboard enforces upon the recruits or the pupils before him a certain series of responses, so we may think of ourselves as enforcing upon our motor centres a series of responses over and over again until they can carry them out without our conscious supervision. Such learning depends upon repetition. It depends also—and this is less generally recognised— upon knowing exactly what movement we want to learn.

The oftener we repeat a movement, the more readily our limbs or fingers fall into it. This applies as much to parts of the movement which are wrong and ineffective as to parts that are correct or skilful. Thus, when a movement is being badly made, practice makes matters worse instead of better. If you go out and practise a golf shot when you are afflicted with a bad attack of slicing or pulling, shanking or topping, you are in effect practising these faults and making them into ineradicable habits. There will be no progress until you are making the right movement instead of the wrong one—and the difficulty is usually to find out what you are doing wrong, and what you ought to do instead. The recruits will not make progress in learning a drill movement under a drill sergeant who does not know what movement he wants them to make.

The guidance of a teacher may be of use. But the teacher, though possessed of the necessary skill, may not know what he does himself. The invention of the cine-matograph made it possible to photograph a movement and reproduce it slowly on the screen for detailed study. It was found that the actual movements made by the skilled workman or the games professional might be different in important respects from what they had themselves supposed. This shows that the ability to make such a skilled movement does not depend upon knowing how it is made. How did such skilled men ever learn such movements without ever knowing what it was that they were learning ? How can we do the like ourselves?

The answer is that we must leave it to our nervous systems to do it for us. It is the motor centres that have to learn how to carry out the movement. They must be given the opportunity to find out for themselves how to do it. The moment in which they do so will be the happy moment in which we " fall into " the new dance step or " get the knack " of handling the unfamiliar implement. A simple experiment may be used to illustrate this.

Let the reader (if not at the moment in a public place, where his action might be open to misconstruction) trace with the forefinger a circle in the air. That is easily done with either hand : one has but to think of the movement as an act one desires to perform and the muscles do the rest. If the reader will consider what is involved in the way of contraction and relaxation of muscles, he will see that it is not such a simple matter as it may appear. When he finds by experiment that he can describe the circle with equal ease in any plane of space—for example, on the wall in front of him, on the table-top, on the ceiling, on his chest, on his back, on the back of the chair on which he is sitting, on the top of his head—he will feel a new respect for the versatility of his motor organisation. He may go on to discover that he may trace his circle just as easily with his forefinger alone, with his hand, with his forearm, with the whole extent of his arm, with his foot, with his leg, with his head, with his tongue against the roof of his mouth, that he may in any of these cases reverse the direction of movement, or substitute a movement of a different shape, such as a cross. He seems to be equipped with the necessary nervous organisation for all these movements.

Let him now try a movement for which one link in the chain of nervous connections is missing. He can describe a circle in front of the body and in the medial plane (that is, at right angles to the line of the shoulders) with either hand and in either direction. Let him try to describe simultaneously such a circle with each hand, but let the two circles be made in opposite directions. He may do it, but this time much more slowly and clumsily ; or his attempt may fail altogether, in which case he will probably feel irritated, perhaps slightly humiliated, and his annoyance may express itself in the judgment that the book and the writer and all this stuff are too silly for words and it would be better to get on to something more sensible. That is how we are apt to feel, when faced with something which we do not do easily, unless we happen to have a very strong motive for mastering it.

Here the motive is an intellectual one : there is nothing to be gained but a little understanding of the processes, by which we learn. As for the feelings of irritation we shall return to them in a later chapter, for they are as grit in the bearings so far as learning is concerned.

If the reader will persist, he will find that he becomes more successful. The movements are less haltingly and clumsily made. They require a less intense concentration of attention. The irritation subsides. Finally, after a sufficient amount of practice, the double movement is made without any effort. Or he may find that he can make nothing of it, that the harder he tries the more impossible it becomes, even that a kind of paralysis seems to take possession of him, so that he makes no movement at all, right or wrong. In either case let him pause to consider the meaning of what he has observed.

Let us suppose the reader to have been successful in mastering the movement. Somehow or other, as a result of taking pains, of making it with close attention and continuous effort, the link that was missing in the chain of nervous connections has been supplied. Before the learning was attempted, there was already in working order the nervous apparatus necessary for making the movement with either hand. Now there has been added the further apparatus necessary for the making of the double movement ; and this is presumably of the nature of a new link between them which controls their joint activity.

The movements of swimming may be taken as an example. In the breast stroke there is a movement to be made by the right leg, while a similar movement is made by the left leg, and these leg movements are to be accompanied by a movement of the right arm and a similar movement of the left arm, which must be so timed as to fit in with one another, to push the body forward through the water and to support it there. This *co-ordination* is brought about by nerve centres at a succession of levels. This is shown schematically in Fig. 2, where each limb is represented by a single muscle for the sake of simplicity, and nervous apparatus for controlling that limb in the swimming-stroke is represented by a single motor nerve. In order that the two arms may work together, the two centres controlling them are linked by motor nerves coming to them from a higher centre. The separate centres for the arms can, so to speak, " do their stuff " on their own, but, if they are to work together and not against one another they must get their cue from the higher centre. A similar link is shown between the two centres controlling the arms. Next, since it is also necessary that legs and arms must work together, a centre at a higher level co-ordinates the movements of legs and arms. Lastly, the centre at the third level is controlled through another motor nerve from a centre in the cortex. This centre is in turn under the control of the sensory centres and so rouses the lower centres to activity when swimming-movements are required.

The whole arrangement is rather like the organisation of an army or of an office or factory. There is a hierarchy, a succession of ranks from the commanding officer to the private, from the managing director to the man at the lathe or the office boy. When the brigade commander desires a certain movement to be made, he explains to his battalion commanders what he wants, and the part that each battalion is to play in the general scheme. Each of these officers then decides how he will carry out his own part of it, and issues instructions accordingly

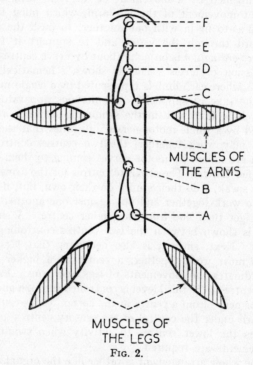

MUSCLES OF
THE ARMS

MUSCLES OF
THE LEGS

FIG. 2.

A, two motor centres, one controlling the movements of each leg; B, motor centre co-ordinating the movements of the two legs; C, two motor centres, one controlling the movements of each arm; D, motor centre co-ordinating the movements of the two arms; E, motor centre co-ordinating the movements of arms and legs; F, motor centre initiating swimming movements, in response to sensory stimulation and/or a conscious decision.

to his immediate subordinates. The company commanders similarly decide how they may best meet his requirements, summon their platoon commanders and detail each for a specific job. These in turn instruct their platoons. When the time for action comes, each platoon moves on the order of its own commander, but in accordance with the general plan.

When the organisation of a business or an office has been built up so that it responds efficiently to the requirements of its executive head, it may be spoken of as an administrative machine. The comparison does it less than justice. A machine, however ingenious, cannot embody any more experience or understanding than its designer has put into it. At best, when he pulls the levers, its working parts will do what he has designed them to do. In contrast, the parts of the administrative machine, the men and women of whom it is composed, have intelligence and experience of their own. Before they can get to work, someone must allot to them their different responsibilities and their different degrees of authority. Someone may have to teach them their jobs. But when they have " shaken down," they are more than cogs in a machine, they are living and learning, and presently they know more about their own jobs than the superiors who have set them to do them, though they may not, as that superior does, understand how these jobs are related to the jobs done by other specialists, or to the plan of the organisation as a whole. There seems to be a somewhat similar relation between the lower and higher nerve centres.

Once a movement has been learned, the lower centres know their job better than the higher centres that give them their cues. In consequence, when we give attention to the subordinate parts of a skilled movement, which is usually performed with success when we leave it to our lower centres, something is quite likely to go wrong. Thus the pianist may begin to miss the notes or the typist the keys, if attention is directed to the tasks of the individual fingers.   Thus the golf drive is likely to be worse instead of better, if we give our attention to what the right wrist or the left heel is doing at the top of the swing, or when the club-head is coming down on the ball. This truth is expressed in the rhyme :

> The centipede was happy quite
>   Until the toad—for fun—
> Inquired which foot came after which.
> He stopped to think : that was the hitch
> That wrought his mind to such a pitch
> He lies distracted in the ditch
>   Considering how to run.*

Until the lower centres have learned their jobs the movement cannot be made comfortably or skilfully. It is as if the superior officer could give only general directions, and his subordinates had to work out for themselves how to act.   That is how we learn skilled movements without knowing exactly how we make them.   That is why, when we want to know exactly what the character of a skilled movement is, we do not ask the skilled craftsman or the games professional what he does, but cinematograph his movements, and then reproduce them slowly in order to study them.

When the movement has been learned, it is only necessary to think of a simple movement as an act to be performed and the nerves and muscles will do the rest.   This applies to all the movements for which we have the necessary nervous apparatus, whether it has been born with us or learned by much practice.   As infants and

---

* I do not know the origin of these lines.   The subject seems to appeal to the poets for there is also a couplet about the water beetle :—
> If he ever stopped to think
> How he did it he would sink

young children we were almost continuously in movement, during waking hours, sometimes to the annoyance of our elders, who would rather have had us sit still and quiet "like good children." This constant movement—waving the arms or legs, playing with the fingers, babbling, creeping, running, jumping, dancing, scribbling, shouting, throwing stones, exploring and examining everything, at first sight so aimless, is really the means by which innumerable movements and variations and combinations of movements have been practised. It is the means by which we have achieved such a command over our bodies, and such ease and versatility of movement.

Such movements involve no effort of the will and no strain upon the attention. They are examples of *ideo-motor action*, that is action in which the *idea* of a movement is immediately followed by the *motor* impulses which bring it about. It is, of course, quite easy to think of such a movement and yet refrain from making it— to think of getting up and yet sit still, to think of bending the forefinger and yet keep it extended. But this is not thinking of the movement as a movement to be performed : it is thinking of the movement, but thinking of it as one not to be performed, or not to be performed immediately ; it is thinking of getting up and at the same time thinking of sitting still, thinking of bending the forefinger and at the same time of keeping it straight.

More striking are those cases in which it is very evident that the idea of the movement is effective in bringing it about in spite of adverse forces. Thus a spectator at a football match, his attention riveted upon one of the players who has the ball at his foot, and excitedly shouting, " Shoot, Jimmie, shoot, shoot ! " may find himself involuntarily performing (to the discomfort of the spectator in front of him) the movement of the leg which his imagination is too vividly portraying for him. Movements of similar origin may be observed in spectators at other games—on the bowling green, for instance —and in the cinema, when, for example, the villain at last receives his deserts and is kicked downstairs.

Sometimes the thought of a movement brings it about even in spite of an active desire that it should not be made. Thus, a novice on a bicycle, who sees a brick or a tin can in front of him, concentrates his attention upon it in fear lest he run into it, and his nerves and muscles necessarily steer the bicycle towards it. He has taken some pains to teach them to do just that ; for, during his novitiate, unable to raise his eyes from the road and look about him, he has kept his gaze on the piece of road just ahead of him and steered towards it, and this steady, inevitable progress towards the obstacle is the measure of his success in doing so. If he would wrest his attention from it, and turn his eyes to the smooth passage upon either side, all would be well. So long as he fails to do so, he feels as if a force not himself is in control of his limbs. By no effort of will can he wrench the handlebars round. The force against which his will is powerless is nothing more or less than the nervous impulses called into action by the idea before his mind. It is quite worth while to explain to someone who is learning to ride a bicycle or drive a car, and who is nervous about meeting traffic, that all he need do is to direct his attention to the piece of road he wants to drive over, instead of to the other vehicle.

Faulty movements in games have often a similar origin. Thus many a golfer may find that to think of slicing is to do it. He cannot make up his mind not to slice without thinking about slicing, and the thought of the act is more potent than the determination to avoid it. Such a player would do better if he would put the fear of slicing out of his mind and concentrate on the thing he wants to do, the despatch of the ball as far as possible straight down the fairway. But the more afraid you are of slicing the more difficult it is to do this. Also this prescription is no panacea to cure all players, since it obviously will not correct fundamental faults of stance, grip or swing.

Many skilled movements are learned like the double movement of tracing two circles in the air in opposite directions. In these cases we carry out the movement with careful attention to each part of it, until we are able to do it without having to think about it so intently. Thus, in learning to typewrite we may begin by making single letters. Anyone can do this by looking for each letter on the keyboard and then pressing the key, but typing a passage in this fashion would be a tedious and unsatisfactory business. Learning to typewrite is learning to strike the right keys in the right order without having to think of the individual letters and the acts of making them. The mind is then free to compose, or to read from a manuscript, the matter that is to be typed. Attention is no longer given to the keys. The subordinate motor centres look after all that. They have become able to do on their own what at first they did only under the direct prompting of the attention and the will.

This comes about slowly. The learner places his fingers over a group of keys and presses them in turn writing the same series of letters over and over again without looking at the keys or his fingers. By and by he can do it smoothly and accurately, and without any feeling of effort. He then practises these letters in different combinations, so that he becomes able to get any one that he wants on that piece of the keyboard. Next he learns a new group of letters in the same way and, when he can do this, he learns to combine letters from the two parts of it. He proceeds in this way until he knows his way about the whole keyboard. Some combinations of letters occur more frequently than others, for example, the letters *tion* at the end of a word. He will soon find that in such cases, instead of having to think of each letter, he can rely on his fingers to pick them out as soon as he thinks of the syllable which they spell. By and by he will deal with whole words in the same way ; and, in course of time, the unit for his attention will no longer be the letter or the syllable, or even the word, but the phrases of which his sentences are built up. Such a hierarchy of typing habits should be compared with the similar hierarchy described in the case of swimming.

Careful studies have been made of students learning to type. These show that progress is not continuous or constant in its rate. It is easy to test the student's speed once a week and plot the result as a graph. It is then found that he may advance rapidly for a time and then for a considerable period no further improvement is visible. He is apt to become discouraged and to think that he has reached the limit of his capacities. This is not so, for, if he continues to practise, there will suddenly come a new period of rapid improvement, to be followed again by a slowing up or even a falling off. What is the explanation ?

It is probable that there is more than one explanation for these " plateaus," as they are called, in the learning curve. One explanation, related to the account which we have been giving of this kind of learning, is that during such periods a habit of a higher order is being acquired. The learner has carried what we may call " letter habits " as far as it is useful to carry them, and he is now learning " syllable habits " or " word habits " or " phrase habits." In such periods the learning is going on but there is for the moment nothing to show for it. It will bear fruit by and by in the rapid increase in speed and ease which are to come. It is important to understand this aspect of learning, for the learner then knows that his efforts are not so barren as they seem, and he does not add discouragement to his other difficulties.

Sometimes it may be a good thing to start with a habit of a higher order. Thus in teaching children to read it is possible to start not with letters but with words, phrases, or even short sentences. There is a good example in learning Morse. Here each letter is represented by a combination of short and long sounds— " dots " and " dashes." The letters may be learned as four " dots," two " dots " and a " dash," and so on. They can be learned by hearing or making the combinations of dots and dashes and thinking of them as the letters, without stopping to analyse them. The learner may then recognise the letters with ease and certainty, although he would have to stop and think if asked what combination of dots and dashes stood for each, just as the expert typist may find the keys he wants infallibly without thinking about it, and yet be unable, without much consideration, to repeat the letters of the alphabet in the order in which they occur in the keyboard. It is like the case of the office or the factory in which the subordinates know the jobs which they are doing better than the superior under whose direction they are doing them.

How then should we proceed in order to learn a new movement, when we have realised that we do not know in detail what we want to learn, and that our nervous organisation must therefore do the learning for us ? The best way to understand this is to carry out another simple experiment. For this the reader will need a mirror, a sheet of paper, a pencil and a piece of cardboard. He should place the paper before him on a table in a position convenient for drawing or writing. The mirror should be placed upright at the head of it, so that the hand, the pencil and the drawing may be seen reflected in it. The card should be held in the left hand between the paper and the eyes, so that the other hand, the pencil and the drawing are concealed by it. The reader may then try to draw a square, and then a diamond, while watching what is happening in the mirror. He should then go on to write a familiar word—*London* or *Psychology* will do—so that it has the appearance of normal writing as seen in the mirror.

He will certainly find all this awkward. That is why it is chosen for the purposes of the experiment. He should not let himself be put off by finding that his pencil behaves in a peculiar manner—as if, indeed, it were possessed of a devil. We have raised this devil expressly for the purpose of studying the ways of such perverse spirits.

A little reflection will reveal the cause of the difficulties. The mirror upsets for us the normal relations between our movements as we see them and as we feel them in our muscles and joints. Thus the movement, which we begin as a movement towards the body, *feels* like a movement towards the body, but it *looks* in the mirror like a movement away from the body. We learned in infancy that certain impulses and muscle and joint sensations went with certain movements taking place before our eyes. The mirror reverses some of these. Thus when we want the pencil to move towards us (in the mirror), we must make the movement and experience the sensations which we expect to accompany a movement in the opposite direction. Learning to draw or write with the mirror means learning a new set of connections between our impulses and muscle and joint sensations on the one hand and our visual experience on the other.

One plan is to work out in our minds what this new set of connections must be, and then deliberately teach this new lesson to our fingers by drilling them in it. This is the plan that worked very well in learning to play the piano and in learning to trace the two circles in the air. It does not work so well here. The reader may try it. He will soon find himself giving it up and trying another. Instead of trying to make the pencil go the way he wants, he will let it start off in whichever direction it may choose. If it goes the wrong way, he will stop it. If it goes the right way, he will let it continue. There will be a great many false starts, but there will soon be some evidence of progress. The pencil less frequently sets out in the wrong direction. It seems to be beginning to know its way about. It is not the pencil that is learning, but the motor centres controlling its movements. The subject began by trying to teach them their business ; now he is giving them the chance to learn it for themselves. If he has the patience to continue the experiment long enough, he will find himself drawing or writing as easily in the mirror as in the ordinary way. Having acquired this new set of habits, he may find, when he returns to ordinary writing, that his pencil is again as perverse as it was when he began the experiment. His new writing habits, learned with the mirror, are now interfering with his normal writing habits. This *interference* is in both cases of the same nature as that found in the experiment used as an illustration in Chapter II.

The experiment has many points of interest. First, there is the question how the improvement takes place. We have here an example of what is called " trial and error " learning. The situation is one in which the subject does not know what to do, the situation being new to him, and must therefore act at random and see what happens. His pencil may set off towards any point of the compass. The chances are therefore against its setting off towards the desired one. If the reader will study his successive attempts he will find that at first the chances seem to be all against its going in the desired direction, but that this gradually changes, until wrong movements drop out, and the right movement is made every time. How does this happen ?

It seems to have something to do with success or failure. When the movement has started we see whether the line is going in the right direction. Every time it does so we are pleased with the success, every time it goes in the wrong direction we are displeased, annoyed, exasperated. For some reason which no one can explain, movements which are successful, and therefore pleasing in their results, are in consequence made more readily on future occasions and wrong or clumsy movements are eliminated. In this way we learn without knowing exactly what it is that we are learning.

It is interesting to consider what may be achieved in this way. A tennis player must return the balls that come into his court by striking them over the net into the territory of his opponent. Each ball comes at a different speed, angle and spin. If we could measure these we could calculate the angle at which the racket should be held and the force with which the ball should be struck in order to place it advantageously in the opponent's court. There is no opportunity of doing this, yet the crack player hits ball after ball with almost infallible accuracy. He has learned by a long process of trial and error—or perhaps we should say that his nervous system has learned for him—to respond to each ball with the appropriate stroke.

There are two rules for this kind of learning. First, the subject must know what he wants to do. He will not improve unless he can see and criticise the results of his efforts. Secondly, he will not improve unless he is trying to do it. A lackadaisical " going through the motions " of some activity will help little towards mastering it. Experiment has shown that cats and dogs can learn to manipulate complicated fastenings in order to get into or out of a box constructed for the experiment when they are induced to do so by tempting food on the other side of the door which is to be opened. They begin with ill-directed, random efforts. If the experiment is repeated on a number of occasions the ineffective movements are gradually dropped out and the animal learns by the same method of trial and error as the subject in the mirror experiment. If, however, an attempt is made to teach the animal by grasping its paws and using them to manipulate the fastenings of the door, little or no learning takes place. Interest is the primary condition of effective learning.

Almost as important is an attitude of mind which is not over anxious. The reader has probably found that to try too hard at this kind of learning defeats its own purpose. He may, for example, have found his writing leaving the line which it should follow and either climbing above or falling below it. The harder he tried to bring it back, the further it would go astray. The explanation of this perversity is simple. Effort can only be effort exerted through the nervous organisation which we possess. When writing in the ordinary way, if the writing tends to go above the line it is necessary to lengthen the strokes made in the direction of one's own body in order to bring it back again. In this case it is necessary to lengthen the strokes made away from the body. But an effort of will enforces the old, inappropriate habit instead of the new and not yet learned one. And so the harder the subject tries, the less successful he is.

If instead he cultivates a more carefree attitude,

letting his pencil move at random, sooner or later the right movement will appear, it will meet with his approval, it will tend to recur more readily and he will feel that he is making progress. We can improve at this kind of learning only by making mistakes. We must therefore feel free to make mistakes and at the same time understand that they do not matter as they will be very quickly eliminated in the " happy moments " when we hit upon the right movement or combination of movements.

Such moments are not at our command. In his experiments on learning, Book found that " The necessary pre-condition for taking a forward step in the learning was effort carefully applied to the work on a good day."[*] On the other hand, "great effort wrongly or carelessly applied is even more detrimental to progress than a simple lapse in attention and effort."[†] The conclusion to be drawn is that :

> . . . if one wants to improve at the most rapid rate, he must work when he feels in good form and likely to succeed, then lounge and wait until it is again profitable to work. It is when all the conditions are favourable that the forward steps or new adaptations are made.

In learning it is not the product of the activity that is of value but the increase in skill, and mere industry and perseverance are not always the quickest means to this, however valuable these virtues may be in the pursuit of routine activities.

---

[*]Q. in Rusk—*Experimental Education*, 1919, p. 220.
[†]Ibid.

Part II

THE GROWTH OF KNOWLEDGE

CHAPTER V

THE GATEWAYS OF SENSE

Item, Two grey eyes, with lids to them ; . . .

. . . . he is beginning the right way, studying the broad effects. It is so easy to lose oneself in details. If you catch the dog, you catch the fleas.

The simplest way of gaining knowledge is through the senses. We *see* that a curtain is blue, that a table is square, that there is a clock on the mantelpiece ; we *hear* that the bell is ringing ; we *taste* the porridge to find out whether there is salt in it ; we *feel* that something is rough or smooth, or hot or sticky ; we *smell* something that is singeing.

In each of these cases the information comes to us through one of our five senses, sight, hearing, taste, smell or touch. It is convenient to have one word for this, which can be used in connection with any of the senses, and the word in use is *perception*. To *perceive* something is to see or hear or taste or smell or touch it, and so become aware of its presence and some of its qualities—its colour, its shape, its position, its sound, its smell, and so on.

Knowledge of this kind comes so easily that at first there seems to be no problem about it. It seems obvious that if a piece of cardboard is red and square and upright and on the mantelpiece, we should at once see that it is

Note.—The quotations at the head of the chapter are from : Shakespeare— *Twelfth-Night*. I, v. 268 ; J. B. Yeats—*Letters*. ed. Hone. 1944, p. 68.

so—that is, granted that we have normal vision and the room is lighted. If it were as simple as this, there would be no problem for the student in connection with perception. It would only be necessary for him to turn the appropriate sense organ upon the object with which he desired to become acquainted and he would perceive it as accurately as the expert.

This is clearly not the case. An expert in phonetics will listen to someone's speech for a few moments and tell him where he spent his childhood, where he went to school and where he has lived since. Each of these environments has left its mark on his speech, though to most of us the slight modifications of vowels or consonants are indistinguishable, even when our attention is directed to them. Mr. Bernard Shaw's professor of phonetics* could pronounce one hundred and thirty distinct vowel sounds, and when his friend, proud of his more modest twenty-four, protested that he could not hear a bit of difference between most of them, the expert replied :

Oh, that comes with practice. You hear no difference at first ; but you keep on listening, and presently you find they're all as different as *A* from *B*.

The layman, feeling someone's pulse may be able to tell that it is beating, and that is about all. The doctor finds the pulse one of the most valuable sources of information about the patient's condition. He has been feeling pulses daily for years, and has learned to discriminate and interpret. Lengthy experience may be necessary. A doctor once remarked to me, while examining a patient's abdomen, that he had been at the job for twenty years before he could rely on what his finger-tips told him. An entomologist will distinguish

* G. Bernard Shaw—*Pygmalion.*

and name some incredible number of ichneumons or beetles. A tea-taster or whiskey-blender will have a correspondingly fine power of discriminating small differences of taste or smell. The expert salesman or craftsman distinguishes equally fine differences in the textiles, or the woods or metals, he handles daily. Little boys will put their elders to shame in recognising a distant aeroplane.

These examples may be taken to show two things. First, that practice can improve our powers of perceiving to a quite remarkable extent ; and secondly, that such improvement is a necessary part of one's equipment in almost any profession or vocation. It is thus worth while to give some attention to it. There is a further reason : not only is perception the simplest mode of gaining knowledge, but it is in some respects typical of all other modes, and so takes us a good step on the way to understanding them also.

It seems natural that we should see the object in front of us or feel the object which is in contact with our fingers, so natural that perhaps it seems a waste of time to pause over anything so obvious. But when we reflect upon it, we may begin to ask how one thing, the mind, can be aware of another thing, the object which is perceived. An early and naive theory supposed that the objects which we see are constantly throwing off small models of themselves (eidola) and that the sense organs are simply tubes (poroi) through which these small models pass into our bodies. This theory shortens the distance between the brain and the object perceived by bringing them into physical contact, but it only makes the real difficulty clear, for contact is not awareness.

We know more about the senses now, though this knowledge leaves the fundamental problem—how one thing can be aware of another thing—as much of a mystery as ever. Thus in the case of sight we know that the object which we see reflects light into the eye, that this light is focused as in a photographic camera on the screen at the back of the eye, that this screen, the retina, consists of sensitive nerve endings which, when stimulated by light, send nervous impulses through the optic nerve to the visual centre at back of the head, and that, when the visual centre is aroused to activity in this way, we see the object in front of us. If there is any break in this chain of events, we do not see the object, or do not see it clearly ; for example, if there is no light, if the lens of the eye is obscured, if the image is not focussed on the retina, if the retina is defective, if the optic nerve is severed, if the visual centre has been destroyed or made inactive.

Thus, the old theory was right at least to this extent, that something does enter the body through the sense organ, but, on the other hand, the something is not in the least " like " the object or our perception of it. A red rose, when I look at it, is not like a ray of light, or a nervous current in the optic nerve, or some kind of nervous process in the visual centre of the brain. In just the same sense a bar of music as heard in the broadcasting studio is not in the least degree " like " the vibrating diaphragm in the microphone, or the wireless waves that carry it to my aerial, or the kind of electrical disturbance it sets up in my wireless set ; but the sounds created by my loudspeaker are undoubtedly " like " the sounds created by the player in the studio. Just as the wireless receiving set produces sounds like those made by the distant player, so, it would seem, the mind creates within itself the perception of the object that stimulates the sense organ. How far the perception is " like " the object for which it stands it is impossible to say. It must have some likeness, or perhaps it would be better to say some correspondence, to it since it enables us to deal with it in an effective way—to see that the nut is tight on the bolt, that the steak is sufficiently cooked, or that someone has misunderstood a casual and flippant remark. But what we perceive is not the object itself : rather it is something created by our own minds on the basis of the cues afforded by the object through the channels of sense.

This conclusion may be supported by the evidence of experiments. These are so devised as to show that our perceptions may be inconsistent with one another— that an object has a different appearance on different occasions, or that it appears differently to different persons. When two perceptions differ like this, both cannot be accurate representations of the same object.

An example will be found in Fig. 3. When the

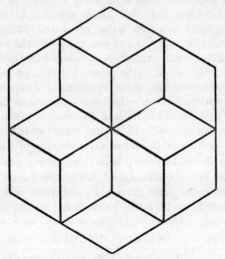

FIG. 3.

reader looks at this figure, it may appear to him either as a six-pointed star inscribed in a hexagon, the whole lying flat in the plane of the paper, or as a three dimensional figure, one cube resting upon two others. If the reader will continue to " watch " it, he will find that it suddenly changes from one of these appearances to the other, or that he sees two cubes above a single one instead of below it. The change comes of itself and is more likely to be facilitated by a passive attitude of mind than by an anxious endeavour to see the figure in a different way. As the reader continues to look at it, the figure will assume now one, now another of these appearances. Since there is no change in the object before him, we must conclude that its different appearances are the creation of his own mind.

The same object may appear differently to two persons. Colour-blindness is an interesting example of this. To normal vision red and green are sharply contrasted colours, and a green letter on a red background is unmistakable. If the red and green are chosen so that they are of equal brightness, a colour-blind person may see no letter at all : the green and the red portions of the field are to him indistinguishable. There is a story of an undertaker's assistant who was colour-blind and, when sent for a black cloth to cover a coffin, brought back a scarlet one.* Black and scarlet were the same to him. A student in one of my extra-mural classes told me that he had recently found that he was colour-blind. He was an accountant and, when the use of coloured inks to distinguish entries for different quarters was introduced into his office, he could not see the point of it. Discussion with his colleagues revealed to him for the first time that to most people red and green ink look

* J. Drever.—Introduction in M. Collins—*Colour Blindness*, 1925, p. xi. From 3 per cent. to 5 per cent. of men are colour-blind.

different. If a note of even loudness be gradually increased in pitch, it will become inaudible at a point some three or four octaves above the highest note of the piano. Some people will hear it quite clearly after it has become inaudible to others, older persons losing it sooner than younger ones. When it has ceased to be heard by human ears a dog will still respond to it—and poachers are said to find a whistle with such a high pitch convenient on some occasions.

Such differences in perception seem to turn upon differences in the efficiency of the sense organ concerned. In the following experiment, which the reader may try for himself, the same person gets contradictory reports from two sense organs simultaneously. Place in a row three small cups or beakers. Fill one with cold water, another with water as warm as is tolerable to a finger immersed in it, and the third with equal quantities of the cold and the hot, so that it is of intermediate temperature. Place the forefinger of one hand in the cold water and the forefinger of the other in the hot water for a minute or two. Then transfer both to the water of medium temperature. This will feel warm to the one finger and cold to the other. In this case the sense organs in the two fingers give opposite reports because they are in different conditions: the one is colder, the other warmer than the water in which it is placed, and, therefore, the one is being warmed, the other cooled by the water round it, and the perceptions obtained through them vary accordingly.

There are other cases in which our perception seems to be biased in a particular direction. An instance of this is to be found in our judgments as to the comparative length of horizontal and vertical lines. Let the reader draw a horizontal line of about one inch in length and then, from a point about the centre of it, draw a vertical

line that looks equal to it. It is a reasonably safe bet
that the latter will be too short, for vertical lines appear
to us longer, and horizontal lines shorter, than they are.

The way in which an object is perceived may be
influenced by its setting. If two lines of equal length be
fitted with arrow-heads as in Fig. 4 so that they are

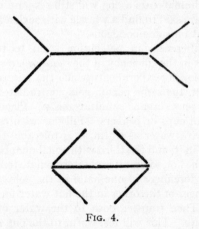

FIG. 4.

turned inward in the one case and outward in the
other, the lines will appear of different lengths. Fig. 5
shows parallel lines which appear to converge because of
the short lines crossing them. A small patch of grey
paper laid upon a sheet of coloured paper will appear to
be tinged with the colour complementary to that of its
background, especially if the whole is covered with and
seen through a sheet of tissue paper. (Red and green
are complementary colours, and so are blue and yellow.)

When the appearance of an object considered by itself
may be so influenced by its setting, it is not surprising
that in a complex whole the parts should be similarly

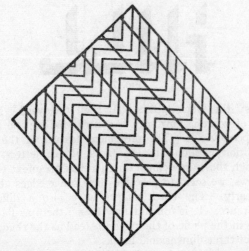

Fig. 5.

Parallel lines which appear to converge. Notice which lines are affected and why.

affected. The black marks in Fig. 6 do not compose such a whole. It is, therefore, easy to study each one separately and to note its shape as a plane rectilinear figure. The same black shapes are reproduced again in Fig. 7, but they are differently arranged. As the reader looks at them they will sooner or later be perceived as a short word printed in block capitals. The black shapes have now a different meaning. They are the shadows

Fig. 6.

FIG. 7.

cast by the block letters that spell the word. Much more of what is now seen is contributed by the mind that perceives it. The prominent feature of the new perception is found in the faces of the letters, and although these are defined only at the edges next to the shadows, we seem to perceive their other edges almost as clearly. The black shapes have also a different appearance. It is difficult now to see them as flat ink marks in the plane of the paper instead as the shadowed sides of three-dimensional blocks.

These meanings are conveyed to our minds only when the black shapes are arranged in a certain way. They depend, that is to say, on certain spatial relations between them, the spatial relations which would be found between the shadows of block letters spelling the word. They depend also upon our apprehending somehow or other that set of relations. We do not do this consciously, saying to ourselves that these three black shapes on the left are similar in shape and in their relative positions to the shadows that would be cast by a block letter H lighted from a point above and to the left. All that we can notice happening in our minds is that the black shapes suddenly come together to form the letters, or perhaps that we suddenly see the letters and not the black shapes as such. It would seem that if our minds can suddenly present us with this interpretation of the pattern of black and white given to us by our eyes, the mental processes involved must have included in some sense the apprehension and recognition of the shapes and spatial relations involved.

That is as it may be. What we can be sure of is that the black marks take on a new meaning when they are seen as parts of a four-letter word. It is now difficult to see them as plane rectilinear figures lying in the plane of the paper. There are two sides to the process. On the one hand, it is only because we see the black marks that we can see the word—there is nothing else on the paper to see. On the other hand, as soon as we see the word the black marks cease to be black marks merely, and appear as parts of the letters forming the word. They are seen as what they are intended to be, only when they are seen as parts of the word.

Examples could be multiplied to illustrate the principle which is involved. That principle may be stated thus :

The perception of a whole is not the sum of the perceptions of its parts taken separately, but includes something more, which alters the way in which the parts themselves are perceived. The something more is the meaning which the whole has when its parts are put together in a certain way, and this meaning of the whole, when it is apprehended, may give to each of the parts a meaning which it did not have when taken by itself.

In Fig. 7 the parts are chosen and arranged to convey a certain meaning. So strong is the tendency of the mind to organise into meaningful wholes whatever is presented to it that we find this tendency operating even in cases where the material presented has not been so arranged. Thus, the outline of a rock or some chance arrangement of the glowing coals in the fire may suggest a face. In Fig. 8 some black squares are arranged at equal distances from one another. As the reader looks at them he will find that they take a certain form or pattern. If he continues to look at them this pattern will presently change to another, and then to another. Thus, the squares may seem to be arranged in horizontal lines, in vertical lines, in diagonal lines, in triangles, in diamonds

FIG. 8.

or squares, in domino fives, as a square and a cross, and so on. Even in the case of such unpromising material our minds seek to impose a pattern of organisation and meaning.

These patterns are more or less familiar ones. They have been learned in the course of our past experience. The easy perception of the black marks as letters is a consequence of our familiarity with the patterns of the letters. In Fig. 9 the black shapes can be seen as the

FIG. 9.

shadows cast by a similar kind of solid object, but its shape is less familiar than that of the letters and it is shown as lighted from below, a less familiar arrangement. It is, therefore, less easy to see as a solid object, though this may be made easier by turning it upside down.

The dependence of perception on learning may be illustrated in another way. There is a test of mental development in its early stages which consists of variously shaped blocks of wood—a cross, a star, a square, a circle, etc.—which fit into recesses of the same shapes in a board. To a normal adult it is at once evident where each of them must go. With a young child or a mental defective it is otherwise. The child of two or three years of age does not immediately recognise the square block as fitting into the square hole, and so on, but can place the pieces in their places only as a result of experiment—perhaps trying the cross in the star-shaped hole, and so on with the others, until it slips into the right one. It is evident that the apprehension of these to us familiar shapes is as difficult for him as, say, the recognition of an algebraical formula as the sum of two squares is to a young student of mathematics.

So strong is the impulse to impose a meaning on what is presented to us that, rather than accept it without a meaning, we frequently impose a false or absurd one where we do not see the real one. Children's mistakes are sometimes of this kind. There is, for example, the story of the child who asked for the hymn about the " baby bear." This proved to refer to the lines* :

> Can a woman's tender care
> Cease towards the child she bare ?

A young child is not interested in the use of maternal affection as a symbol of the constancy of Divine Love.

---

*Wm. Cowper—*Olney Hymns* 19.

But he is interested in child she-bears. Thus interest as well as previous experience plays a part.

In this case we have a pattern not of visual forms but of words. The same principles apply and are therefore relevant to all studies carried on through the medium of words. Here, again, we are concerned with meaning : it is the function of words to convey meaning from one mind to another. This time the words are the parts, and the sentences, paragraphs or chapters in which they are arranged are the wholes. Let us see how the principles already stated apply to words.

Consider the following sentence :

Her face is hard.

Four words placed together convey a certain meaning and it is clear that this is in the main the putting together of the meanings which the two words " face " and " hard " would bear if taken separately. But suppose we add two more words :

Her face is hard to describe.

The meaning of the statement is now altered, and this alteration turns on two consequences of the new company in which " hard " finds itself. First, it has attached itself to " to describe " instead of to " face," and, secondly, in this new partnership it means not " unsympathetic " but " difficult." Thus " hard," the part, chameleon-like, changes its colour to suit its background. When we have noted this versatility, we may go on to notice that in the first example also the meaning has been modified by the context from the simple meaning (as in " Diamonds are very hard ") to a less usual one. It is true that the meaning of a sentence depends upon the words of which it is made up. But it is also true that the meaning of a word depends upon the sentence in which it is placed.

Walter Leaf tells how,* on reading Swinburne's poem *Aholibah* for the first time he came to the line :

> Wool whereon live purple bleeds. . . .

and looked up and said " What on earth are bleeds ? I never heard of such things." " Live " may be either a verb or an adjective and " purple " may be either a noun or an adjective.   Reading the words one at a time, we are likely to take " live " and " purple " as verb and adjective respectively, and then expect a noun, which will be qualified by the one and play the part of the subject of the other.   But " bleeds " will not fit into this scheme.   This is not how we usually read.   We do not settle the meanings of individual words until we have grasped the whole grammatical unit, in this case until we have got as far as " bleeds," which determines that " live " and " purple " must play their parts as an adjective and a noun.   Occasionally, as in this little incident, the whole fails to determine as it should the meanings to be given to the parts of which it is composed. Then, if the parts admit of another interpretation, that interpretation may be placed upon them, however incongruous it may be, as when the schoolboy rendered Horace's line :

> Post equitem sedet atra cura,

as " After riding the dark lady sits down with care."†

Not only a word but a phrase or a sentence may play the chameleon in this fashion.   A familiar example is the line :

> For Brutus is an honourable man ; . . .

and its variants which recur in Mark Antony's speech over Cæsar's body with a continual change of meaning

---

* C. M. Leaf—*Walter Leaf*, 1932, p. 96.

† Odes, III, I, 40. It may be rendered: "Black Care sits at the horseman's back."

as the speaker works upon and reverses the sympathies of his audience.

There are four words in Shakespeare's *Hamlet* which have perhaps been as much praised as any four words in literature. They are :

> The rest is silence.

Taken by itself this is only a rather portentous and affected way of saying :

> That's all I can tell you.

Its effectiveness—for its effectiveness is not in dispute—comes from its setting. Outwardly the play tells of a prince, disinherited by a palace intrigue, who dies in an unsuccessful attempt to reassert himself. Actually the drama which engages our attention takes place in Hamlet's mind : it is a story of conflicting motives and ideals, and it is this spiritual conflict that excites our breathless interest. The tragedy may be said to culminate when death brings this conflict to an end, unresolved and unrevealed to men. The words quoted are thus the very climax of the story and charged with an emotional intensity to which every preceding scene has contributed. Taken by themselves they are unremarkable, except for their somewhat stilted diction, which may be regarded as a deliberate stylization, used to draw attention to them, and so facilitate the discharge through them of the slowly accumulated electrical charge of the play.

There is an even more surprising example of this principle in the last scene of Shakespeare's *King Lear*—the reiteration of one familiar disyllable to form a complete line :

> Never, never, never, never, never !

perhaps the most overwhelming in all tragedy. To see

that it owes its force to its setting, it is only necessary to consider how weak, or even absurd, it would sound if it appeared in the first scene instead of in the last.

The most striking play made with the shifting meaning of a single word in different contexts is perhaps the traditional conjuring with *malo*, which may be put in dialogue form :

1st Speaker : Construe : *Malo malo malo malo*.
2nd Speaker : It can't be done. Try it yourself.
1st Speaker : *Malo*, I would rather be,
            Malo, in an apple tree,
            Malo, than a bad boy,
            Malo, in adversity.

The repetition of the word does not, of course, suggest these four meanings, yet, in a suitable context, it may bear a sense corresponding to any one of them. Thus :

Malo pius quam dives esse—I would rather be good than rich.
Puer, in malo sedens, poma est—Sitting in an apple-tree, the boy eats apples.
Bonus puer divis gratior malo est—The good boy is more pleasing to the gods than the bad boy.
Æquam serva mentem in bono et malo—Keep an even mind in good fortune and in adversity.

CHAPTER VI

THE WEB OF THOUGHT

When a man thinketh on any thing whatsoever, His next Thought after, is not altogether so casuall as it seems to be.

Some things are so connected in our minds that, when our attention is drawn to one of them, the other is at once thought of : David—and Jonathan ; Swan—and Edgar ; bacon—and eggs. Such items are connected in our minds because we have previously met them together, and this connection is called *association*. The one item is so tied or associated to the other that, when it comes into our consciousness, it may drag the other after it.

Since our experience is continuous during our waking life, every item of our experience must be connected in this way with what came before it, or came with it, or came after it. Thus, the web of association, woven of innumerable strands, should comprise all that has ever happened to us—everything that we have seen or heard, or felt, or thought, or imagined, or feared, or hoped. Things are not quite so simple as this, and the laws of association do not explain so much as they were once believed to do, but they are still useful conceptions.

The cortex consists, as we have seen, of an enormous number of connecting nerve fibres. Is not the web of associations the mental counterpart of this equally intricate physical network ? It is tempting to think of each mental item—each *idea*—as corresponding to some little piece of nervous organisation, and then to suppose

Note.—The quotation at the head of the chapter is from Thomas Hobbes—*The Leviathan*, Pt. I, c. iii. Fveryman's Library.

that the associations between the ideas correspond to nerve fibres joining these nervous units. When one of the nervous units becomes active, the corresponding idea appears in consciousness, and at the same time some of the nervous energy generated tends to flow along the connecting fibre to the other unit. When that is awakened in turn, the corresponding idea comes to mind.

Some parts of the brain have been found to control particular parts of the body—to move the arms, the legs, the speech organs, etc. Other parts of the cortex—the so-called " silent " areas—are not found to have any such motor function. These have been named the *association areas*. Much of this is speculation. No one has ever seen the brain mechanisms in operation. But the parallel is certainly suggestive, and there is evidence that supports it. Thus, an injury to the brain may result in the loss of abilities which have been learned, and the patient may be found relearning as an adult the spelling and arithmetic of his school-days from the same kind of school-books and by much the same methods.

Since every experience which we have is woven into the same web of association, it would seem that every idea we possess must be linked to every other idea, and that it should, therefore, be possible to proceed from any item of our past experience to any other. This is not quite the case, for our thoughts turn more readily in certain favoured directions than in others, and some things which we should like to recall elude us altogether. The minds of normal people are taken up with something that is to be done or arranged or contrived or discovered. They do not wander at random along the paths of association. But something like this happens in abnormal circumstances—in delirium, in insanity, in extreme fatigue, in senility, or when we relax and let our thoughts ramble where they will.

It is easy to study such mental rambling and to see how far it supports this conception of the web of association. Take some familiar idea—*Christmas, Parliament, aeroplane* or *toothache.* Starting from it, let the thoughts go where they will. Then note the course they have taken, and try to account for their direction. With this method successive items may come to the mind as mental pictures of people or places, or they may come as words. Another method confines the memories to words. In this case the subject starts from any familiar word and writes down, or gets someone else to write down, the words which it suggests, one following upon another.

In the former experiment it should be easy to account for some of the transitions in terms of previous occasions on which the items have been met with together. Thus *Christmas* may remind you of a place in which you once spent Christmas, then of someone met in that place, or something that happened in it, and so on. Sooner or later it will become evident that this explanation, true so far as it goes, is not the whole story. It will be found that the thoughts will be drawn towards topics connected with your stronger interests, or that they will turn aside from what is unpleasant to recall. Each new association brings you, as it were, to a cross-roads where there are several paths to choose from, and interest determines which path your thoughts will take.

In the second experiment we may find links in either the sounds or the meanings of the words. Thus *father* may suggest *rather, master faster,* and *nut hut,* because of the similarity of sound. *Father* may suggest *mother, master servant, nut bolt,* because the one implies the other. Or we may have *black* followed by *white, high* by *low, war* by *peace,* in virtue of opposition or contrast of meaning. The relation may be causal—*poison death, injure hate, kiss well.* It may be that of whole and part—*jug handle, car wheel, England Devon.* It is interesting to collect a few score of such associations from one's own mind or someone else's, and then try to classify them under such headings.

Three conclusions which are likely to be suggested by such an attempt may be mentioned :—

First, it is impossible to tell in any such case what the nature of the link has been, unless we have the report of the subject with whom we are working. Thus *war* may have suggested *peace* because these terms are opposites, or *war* may have brought to mind Tolstoi's *War and Peace* in which the two words are linked, or *war* may have brought to mind the risk of war and the subject's desire for peace. The causes determining the particular response which we get may be deeply rooted in our subject's past experience. A method similar to this is, therefore, commonly used in exploring the mind of a patient in need of mental treatment and by this means it may be possible to find out the causes of his symptoms and suggest means of helping him.

Secondly, we find many instances in which the link seems to be some logical relation—similarity, oppositeness, cause and effect, part and whole. Things so related will frequently come to our notice together, and so it is not easy to say how far they have been linked in our minds because of their logical relation to one another, and how far because of their being brought to our notice together. *Black* and *white* are opposites. But we have also black ink and white paper, black and white dominoes, black evening clothes and white shirt, " put it in black and white," " don't argue that black is white," and so on.

Thirdly, it will be found that, when the thoughts are allowed to wander, they do not altogether follow random paths. In either of the two experiments suggested the reader is likely to find particular topics—his dominant interests—obtruding themselves, and other less welcome topics—this may not be so easy to observe—getting the go-by, the cold shoulder.

The second and third conclusions are important, for, if our trains of thought were obliged to follow a succession of ideas determined by the accidents of our experience, they could serve no purpose—they would be as useless as the incoherent maunderings of delirium. Sometimes our thoughts do follow such casual paths and errors result. Thus, the student who asserted that " King Alfred the Great translated *Adam Bede* into English " had two associations to *Bede*, the title of George Eliot's novel and the Venerable Bede whose Latin chronicle King Alfred is said to have translated into Anglo-Saxon. The schoolboy, who, when asked to write a note on the Diet of Worms, declared it to be " what Christ ate in the desert," presumably did not know the word *diet* in the sense of a conference or *Worms* as a town, and, clutching at any suggestion that offered, mixed up St. John's locusts and wild honey with the Temptation in the Wilderness.

We can exercise control over the kind of word which is to come to mind. Thus, beginning with *hat*, the reader may call to mind a series of articles of apparel, or beginning with *chair*, a number of articles of furniture. Appropriate words will suggest themselves without his consciously choosing them. If he seeks the opposite of *black, high, short, warm, dry, sweet, loud, broad, talkative, friendly, easy,* the appropriate word will come in each case. This is how we get the word or idea which we need in the case of a problem of thought or action. Thus a broken string may suggest a piece of window cord because it will prove stronger, or a raincoat may be put aside for a mackintosh because the latter is more waterproof, or *musico* may suggest *Boucicault, quackery Thackeray, Peveril Sacheverell,* and *Daniel Defoe Mr. Guizot,* if what is wanted is a series of rhymes.* In these cases the idea that comes to mind is one that bears a certain relation to the idea that we already have before us, and this relation is one which is determined by the purpose we have in view.

This is the serious use of associative links. In other connections we may treat them more flippantly, and a teacher, addressed in public as Mr. Davis-Locker may be known when out of earshot as " the Abyss, the Depths of the Ocean, the Sailors' Cemetery, the Skeleton's Home," and allusively referred to when on the warpath by citing Victor Hugo :

> Enfin l'abîme se décida à livrer combat.

It is a game we all play at.†

Nevertheless, when, as students or teachers, we wish to make use of the principles of association, it is usually to that stated at the beginning of this chapter that we appeal—we assume that if two things have been seen or heard or thought of together, either will in future lead to the recall of the other, and so we present together the items between which we wish to establish connections. The child is made to repeat the arithmetical tables, until he can " say " them. He learns lists of capes and bays, or towns and manufactures, or kings and dates, he repeats grammatical definitions or grammatical rules or lists of exceptions, he learns by heart the Catechism or a piece of verse. In all these cases the technique of learning is the same—the items are repeated in a fixed order, so that a chain of associations may be formed which will hold them together. Then any item may be recovered from the abyss of memory by pulling on the chain till it comes to the surface.

---

*W. S. Gilbert—*Patience* Act I.

†C. G. Crump—*The Red King Dreams,* 1931, pp. 168-9.

How should one set out to establish such a chain ? Much attention has been given to this problem, which is one that lends itself to experimental study. The results of these inquiries, in so far as they have a practical bearing on the work of a student, will be referred to in a later chapter on memory. At this point it is more important to note the limitations of this kind of learning, and to point to more valuable mental powers which it ignores.

A chain of associations is like any other chain—its strength is that of its weakest link. If I can repeat the names and dates of the Kings of England in their order, and if I want to use this accomplishment to find the dates of Henry VII, I begin to pull in my chain link by link. Now if any one of these links fails—if I stick at Henry II, for instance—all that comes after is lost. If, on the other hand, the dates of Henry VII's accession and death are woven into a context of other facts and dates of his period, they are less likely to be lost and, if the actual year cannot be recalled with certainty, there is a guarantee against gross error, which does not exist in the other case. It is the difference between a rigmarole and a piece of systematised knowledge. This is not an argument against knowing the dates of the English kings and being able to reproduce them in order. Such a set of dates forms a useful chronological backbone, a main structural feature in such a systematic organisation as has been advocated, but it should be learned as part of such a context, for it is as little use without it as an index is without the text to which it refers.

The names *linear association* and *systematic association* may be given to these two ways of organising material which has to be remembered. The difference between them may be shown in diagrammatic form. In Fig. 10 the small circles represent the items to be learned, the

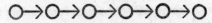

FIG. 10.

horizontal lines represent the associative links between them. It is clear that if one of these links is broken all that lies beyond it is lost. In Fig. 11 the circles are arranged so that each is linked to the others in more than one way. If one link fails, another may hold.

Instead of using the metaphor of the chain we may think of the structure as a group of nerves in the cortex. In this case the separate items (corresponding to the small circles) are brain centres, and the lines are nerve fibres connecting them. What happens when we seek to recall one item of knowledge corresponding to one of these nerve centres ? When we think of an item connected with it, a nervous impulse flows from the corresponding centre to the one we desire to make active, and the required item appears in our minds. This is, as was said above, speculation, for no one can watch the brain centres at work, but it seems a reasonable explanation. Now, the more paths there are from the one centre to the other the more likely it is that the attempt will be successful.

It sometimes happens that we wish to recall a particular item—a name, an address, a telephone number.

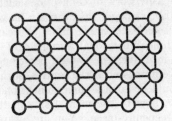

FIG. 11.

It refuses to come. Or one which is obviously the wrong one obtrudes itself every time. The greater the effort made to remember, the less success there is. Very often the best thing to do is to relax the effort and let the mind dwell on any other items relevant to the topic that can be recalled—the friend's face, his voice, the last place in which we saw him, the book he borrowed, the card he sent, some mutual acquaintance. The chances are that while we are doing this the required item will suddenly present itself. This also can be illustrated by a diagram of nerve centres and connections. In Fig. 12 X stands for the wanted item and the circles for memories connected with it. The arrows show the direction of

Fig. 12.

nervous impulses set up when the memories corresponding to the circles are brought to mind. The more of them there are, the stronger the effect produced at X.

Let us return to our metaphor of the chain. It will be clear that a network of connections such as that in Fig. 11 would be stronger than a chain, in which everything depends on each single link. We can go a step further : a three-dimensional arrangement—more difficult to show in a diagram—would be stronger still. A group of nerve fibres and nerve centres, such as we have supposed, would be such a three-dimensional structure.

Let us turn now to the mental side of the problem. Look at a threepenny-piece. You are aware at once of the flat sides, the colour of the metal, the three thrift flowers, the inscription, and the date. You are aware at the same time of the relations between these—aware that the inscription is round two-thirds of the circumference, above and to the sides of the flowers, that the date is underneath, and so on. Your attention passes as freely from the flowers to the sides, or to the date, as to the description or the colour. This is much more like our three-dimensional structure than like the chain or even the plane figure. Why do we ever take the chain as our model in learning ? Why do we try to set out the items of our experience in single file ?

There is a simple explanation. What is communicated from one mind to another is communicated mainly in words, and words, whether spoken or printed, must be set out in a row. Thus communication does violence to the complexities and intricacies of our thoughts. The speaker or the writer is put to the trouble of forcing his complex and many-sided matter into a simple straight line ; what he perceives or grasps in one comprehensive mental act must be dissected and rearranged like a square linen sheet cut into strips to make a rope. Thus, to go back to the threepenny-piece, the inscription, the flowers, the date, the relation of the inscription to the flowers, the relation of the date to the flowers, and so on, must all be separately mentioned, one after the other, instead of being grasped simultaneously ; and they must be set out in one particular order, though any other order may be equally appropriate. The hearer, or reader, must then take this sequence of bits and pieces and put its elements together for himself, so as to re-create in his own mind the complex pattern, with its many interrelations between the items, to which the linear arrangement has done violence.

What we learn for ourselves from our practical experience is not arranged in our minds chain fashion.

The farmer knows his fields and woods this way and that,
so that he can cross from one point to another without
stopping to think how he must go ; and he can go back
and forward in time in thinking of rotation of crops, past
and future, draining done or to be done, successive
accretions of buildings, house and cottages and barns.
The engineer has the different parts of his engine simultaneously in mind when he is trying to locate some fault :
he does not have to follow the order of topics adopted in
some text-book.   Knowledge for use does not have a
linear arrangement in the memory.   It is only when
knowledge has to be communicated that it must move
like an army on the march in column of route—a forma-
tion which has no military value except as a means of
passing from one area of deployment to another.

The art of writing is largely the art of imposing this
linear order upon more or less recalcitrant material.   The
art of reading is largely the reconstruction of a multi-
dimensional structure from a linear one.   A good writer
presents his material so as to facilitate this reconstruction.   He must paint in successive strokes, but he may
nevertheless set out his successive items in such a way as
to suggest something more than a linear pattern.
Consider this description of the entry to the Thames as
it appeared in the 'sixties and 'seventies of last century :

Every quarter of an hour the imprint and the
presence of man, the power by which he has transformed nature, become more visible ; . . .   From
Greenwich the river is nothing but a street a mile
broad and upwards, where ships ascend and descend
between rows of buildings, interminable rows of a dull
red, in brick or tiles bordered with great piles stuck
in the mud for mooring vessels, . . .   To the west,
rises an inextricable forest of yards, of masts, of
rigging : these are the vessels which arrive, depart or

anchor, . . . massed against the chimneys of houses and the pulleys of warehouses, with all the tackle of incessant, regular, gigantic labour. A foggy smoke penetrated with light envelopes them ; and the brackish, tawny, half green, half violet water. balances in its undulations striking and strange reflections. . . . Nothing is natural here, . . . But the hugeness of the conglomeration and of the human creation hinders us from thinking about this deformity . . . for want of pure and healthy beauty, the swarming and grandiose life remains ; . . .*

First a general idea, man's transformation of nature, provides the matrix in which the items find their places. Then comes the broad framework of the visual picture, the broad river transformed to a street. Successive details are given their places in this framework. In order that the unity of the whole may not be lost, all are shown as enveloped in the same luminous fog. Finally we return to the impression of vast human energy. Helped by these devices, we construct a picture which remains before the mental eye as we read, and so the total impression is that of a unified whole in which the various parts have their places. There is an analogy in the mechanical process by which the scanning apparatus used in television breaks up the picture into a temporal succession of varying brightnesses, and the receiving apparatus presents these with an appearance of simultaneity. The more work an author puts into his writing, the more likely he is to perform a similar miracle in the mind of his reader.

I said : " A line will take us hours maybe :
Yet if it does not seem a moment's thought,
Our stitching and unstitching has been naught.†

---

* H. Taine—*Notes on England;* 6-8, q. in Arthur Bryant—*English Saga,* pp. 153-4.
† W. B. Yeats—*In the Seven Woods,* " Adam's Curse."

But one-half of the miracle is worked by the mind of the reader.

The art of study, when it is directed to printed material, is largely the art of reconstructing in one's own mind the pictures, thoughts or emotion patterns which the writer has sought to convey through the medium of words. To do this we must grasp each unit as a whole and understand the complex and intricate ways in which all its parts are inter-related : it is not enough to direct attention to the order in which they are set out and seek to retain them as a chain of linear associations. This may sound formidable. It is not really so. It is what we do spontaneously with any material which commands our interest—a novel, an anecdote, a cinema film or the description of a machine or other structure connected with our daily activities or hobbies. Interest means more than this power of reconstruction, for it involves also a motive for using it. Both must be present, if what is being studied is to be grasped and retained.

The student's conscious aim is probably to remember what he reads. This is an endeavour which frequently defeats his own ends, for to aim at remembering something comes very near to being afraid that we shall forget it, and such fears have a nasty habit of ensuring their own justification. The student's aim should rather be to understand what he reads, for what we understand and are interested in is likely to stick to us. After we have grasped the meaning of a piece of writing it maybe useful to go back upon it and make special arrangements for its efficient recall when the need for it arises. This is a subject to which we must return. Here we may emphasise this dependence of recall upon understanding, and of understanding upon the grasp of successive units as complex wholes composed of inter-related parts, by comparing from this point of view two short passages of prose.

The first of these will be found on p. 87 headed " The Admiral." If the reader has already looked at it, he should now try to put on paper as much of it as he can recall. If he has not seen it, he should turn to it now, and read it through once at his ordinary reading speed, and then try to reproduce it. The second passage, " Brother Yves," will be found on p. 88. If it has been seen already, try to reproduce as much of it as possible. If it has not been seen, read as before and try to reproduce. This is not a test of your powers of memory, and it should not be approached with anxiety as to the result. It is a test of the two passages, from the point of view of the impression which they make on the mind. It is the two pieces of prose that are on their trial, not you. The trial should be made, if possible, before reading the next paragraph, in order that your own observations may not be prejudiced by the comments about to be made.*

There will, I think, be no doubt about the result of the comparison. Reproduction of the first passage depends upon verbal or " parrot " memory ; that is, memory which is independent of any grasp of the meaning—for the simple reason that there is no meaning to grasp. Reproduction of the second passage turns upon grasping the structure of a simple anecdote and, if this is grasped—that is, if the reader has seen the point of the story—the essentials of the passage are likely to be reproduced, even if the order of some of the parts is altered or some of the wording is changed.

Now there is no doubt as to the comparative usefulness of these two types of memory. There are purposes for which verbal memory is useful, and there are persons who

* The first passage was constructed for the purposes of this experiment. The second passage is adapted from Joinville's *Chronicle of the Crusade of St. Lewis*. tr. Sir Frank Marzials. Everyman's Library.

possess a special talent for it. But words which have little meaning for us are for the most part a useless burden. Perhaps their only value is to be found in the examination room, where a student may attempt by this means to " kid " an examiner into granting him a certificate of competence to practise something for which he is unfit. On the other hand, where the meaning has been grasped, that meaning can be applied when circumstances arise in which it is applicable, or suitable words can be found in which to restate it in the examination-room.   There are of course circumstances in which we want both the meaning and the exact words—in literature, particularly verse, and in quoting, particularly a legal document, or a position taken up by a scientific or philosophical writer— but in these cases we want the exact words as the only means to getting the exact meaning, and it is better to go for this to the printed text and not rely upon the memory.

We may now consider the characteristics of the second passage which are favourable to recall. It is a single anecdote with a point to it. In such an anecdote everything is subordinated to making the point. Thus, the omission of any necessary part of such a story would be evident even to someone who heard it for the first time. On the other hand, such a story may include items which are not essential parts of its structure but have value as giving verisimilitude or local colour.* To read such a story and to see the point of it, is to be able to reproduce its essential structure.   Changes in the subordinate

---

* Two such redundancies have been omitted from the version used for the experiment.   In the chronicle the story begins with the words " While they were going from their hostel to the palace of the soldan, Brother Yves saw an old woman going across the street, . . ."   When the anecdote is taken from its setting, the occasion and place of the meeting and the name, Brother Yves, do not contribute to its point. Similarly, if, in reproducing it, one inserts such " corroborative detail, intended to give artistic verisimilitude to an otherwise bald and unconvincing narrative " these additions may be harmless or even helpful.   Sir Walter Scott once remarked that he could not retell a story without "giving it a new hat and stick," and that was, no doubt, what he meant.

details, such as placing the meeting in a street or on a country road, or putting the water into a jug instead of a bottle, or into the right hand instead of the left, are clearly of little importance.

Not only does the anecdote have a point, it has a structure. In this case the structure is a very simple one. The old woman's action arouses curiosity. Curiosity leads to a question. The answer raises a second question. A second answer completes the incident. It is a simple and unmistakable pattern.

Through this there runs a symmetrical pattern of ideas :

right	..	left
fire ..	..	water
burn	..	quench
paradise	..	hell
reward	..	fear

It is a pattern in which one item implies another, so that instead of carrying each as a dead-weight on the memory, we may be uncertain how much we reproduce as an act of recall and how much as a act of re-creation. Thus in reproducing material in which there is this kind of inter-dependence of the parts, we do not reproduce mechani-cally, but by mental processes of the same kind as those by which the writer's mind produced the material originally. The example used here is a literary one, but it is in the case of philosophical, scientific and technical studies that this principle has its most complete application.

Consider from this point of view the passage* printed on page 89. If the reader is unacquainted with Spencer's philosophy, he may find this as difficult to reproduce as the passage made up of unrelated phrases. This is because he does not see the point of it. Actually its parts

---

*Herbert Spencer—*First Principles*, Part II, Chapter XXII, *ad. fin.*

are as coherent, as inter-dependent as the parts of the anecdote from Joinville. The reader may be ready to suggest that it is more difficult to understand. In other words, the passage may have such unity of meaning, but that unity is not evident to him. Why ? The anecdote is addressed to and should be at once grasped by any mind acquainted with Christian ideas as to moral goodness and the love of God. The paragraph from Spencer is addressed to the reader who has progressed through the previous chapters of Spencer's book and so prepared himself for understanding it. Approached with such understanding, it is probably not more difficult to grasp and recall than the anecdote. But there is this difference —our whole experience of life in a Christian community has prepared us to understand the one, whereas the time most of us have given to the study of the Synthetic Philosophy is more limited.

We may now compare the results of this experiment with those of the experiment based on Figs. 6 and 7 (pp. 59-60.). In both cases they turn upon the relations between a whole and its parts. The meaning of the whole—in this case the point of the anecdote—gives meaning to the parts by making each an essential part of that whole. If the reader had tried to memorise the black shapes in Fig. 6 and to reproduce them, it would have been necessary to memorise each shape separately and to give separate attention to each feature of each shape. In redrawing them, it would then have been easy to make mistakes and impossible to check these without reference to the original drawing. Even then the comparative sizes of some of the parts would probably have been in doubt. When the same shapes are re-arranged in Fig. 7, the problem of memorising and reproducing them is altogether changed. It is merely necessary to recall that the shapes make the word HILL and that they are the shadows cast by these letters. They can then be reproduced without difficulty. Because the whole implies the parts and their inter-relations, it is only necessary to recall the whole in order to be able to supply the parts which it implies.

So natural is it to us to unify, that, as we saw in the case of Fig. 8, we impose patterns that have no objective justification upon the objects that we perceive. Upon the same principle whatever our minds produce has some structural unity. The passage on p. 87 was specially constructed to exclude as far as possible significant relations between its parts, yet, if the reader will look at it again, he will see that this attempt was not wholly successful, for *port* is relevant to *Admiral*, *number* to *motor accidents*, *motor accidents* and *beginning* to *black-out*, *increase* to *frequency*, *last year* to *films*, and *Canterbury* no doubt suggested *diocese*, and *no explanation* a minister of state at question time, and therefore *temporary expediency*. It is difficult to write pure nonsense, for the nature of our minds is such that sense " keeps breaking in." The reader may find it interesting to try to construct such a passage for himself, and to note whether he is more successful in excluding all significant relations from it.

This unifying process works at successive levels. A word is a group of letters. A sentence is a group of words. A paragraph is a sequence of sentences. Successive paragraphs make a chapter and successive chapters a book. Each of these—word, sentence, paragraph, chapter—is a whole in which its subordinate parts are unified, and a part, which with other like parts is united in the next larger whole in this hierarchy. It follows, that, to comprehend the subordinate units, we must comprehend the larger ones—that we must know the book as a whole, before we can appreciate the parts of which it is composed or, in more familiar language, that it is easier to read a book if you know what it is about. Sometimes the writer in his preface or introductory chapter tries to give the reader such a bird's-eye view of the whole argument. Sometimes it must be sought elsewhere—in an editor's introduction, in an account of the author's life, in a history of the subject. Sometimes the reader must obtain it for himself—by studying the table of contents, by skimming, by looking first at the summaries, sometimes provided at the ends of the chapters. As a last resort he must read the book through to see what it is about, as the only available means of fitting himself to read it with profit. But he must not expect this first reading to be very fruitful or satisfying.

THE ADMIRAL

The Admiral of the West Port, addressing the Finance Committee at Canterbury, complained that the number of elephants given away in motor accidents in his diocese, between the beginning of the black-out and last year's deficit, had led, in spite of an increase in the frequency of split infinitives in the new tractors now used for the diagnosis of imaginary numbers between the seams of last year's films, and other small numerical opportunities for displacing the pages in logarithmic succession, to no alteration during the period for which no explanations were attributed to temporary expediency.

BROTHER YVES

He saw an old woman who bore in her right hand a
dish full of fire, and in her left a bottle of water. He
asked her : " What are you going to do with these ? "
She answered that with the fire she meant to burn up
paradise, so that nothing might be left of it, and with the
water she meant to put out the fire of hell, so that nothing
might be left of it. He asked : " Why do you want to
do this ? " She replied : " Because I would have it
that no one will do good in order to win the reward of
paradise, or avoid evil because of the fear of hell, but
only for the love of God, who is good and can give us
what is best for us."

EVOLUTION

Thus, from the persistence of force follow, not only the various direct and indirect equilibrations going on around, together with that cosmical equilibration which brings Evolution under all its forms to a close, but also those less manifest equilibrations shown in the readjustments of moving equilibria that have been disturbed. By this ultimate principle is provable the tendency of every organism, disordered by some unusual influence, to return to a balanced state. To it also may be traced the capacity, possessed in a slight degree by individuals and in a greater degree by species, of becoming adapted to new circumstances.

CHAPTER VII

DETECTION WITHOUT CRIME

" You know my methods, . . . Watson."

" I am inclined to think——" said I.
" I should do so," Sherlock Holmes remarked impatiently.

Mr. Hesketh Pearson, in his biography of Conan Doyle, remarks that there are only two other characters in English literature whose names are as familiar to the man in the street as that of Sherlock Holmes.

> Any coal-heaver, docker, charwoman or publican would recognise what was meant by . . . "a regular Romeo" or "a blasted Shylock" or "a bleeding Sherlock Holmes."

Thus, Sherlock Holmes has become the personification of the power of thought. The Scotland Yard bungler may be nonplussed, or he may rush into precipitate and misdirected action. For the great detective thought comes first.

> ". . . I must be prompt over this matter."
> "What are you going to do then?" I asked.
> "To smoke," he answered. "It is quite a three-pipe problem, and I beg that you won't speak to me for fifty minutes."*

He curled himself up in his chair and sat there with his eyes closed, so that Watson thought that he had dropped asleep. By and by, when he had solved his problem he suddenly sprang out of his chair with the gesture of a man with his mind made up and ready to act.

Note.—The quotations at the head of the chapter are from : Conan Doyle—
" The Crooked Man," in *The Memoirs of Sherlock Holmes; idem—The Valley of Fear.*
  * *Idem*—" The Red-Headed League," in *The Adventures of Sherlock Holmes.*

Thought is itself the most important kind of action
and Mr. Peter Jones, the efficient police agent, may be
" as brave as a bulldog, and as tenacious as a lobster if
he gets his claws upon anyone " and yet " an absolute
imbecile in his profession."* The popularity of Sherlock
Holmes is thus a symbol of the public recognition of the
importance of thought.

This importance is not limited to the solution of the
ever engrossing problem of Hoo-dun-it ?

> To draw inferences has been said to be the great
> business of life. . . . The business of the magistrate,
> of the military commander, of the navigator, of the
> physician, of the agriculturalist, is merely to judge of
> evidence, and to act accordingly ; . . . and as they
> do this well or ill, so they discharge well or ill the duties
> of their several callings.†

Not only do our powers of thinking determine the
effectiveness of our actions in all ordinary affairs of life
which are not matters of routine, but powers exactly
similar, though perhaps greater in degree, have created
the science, scholarship and philosophy which are the
material of our studies. These powers of thought are,
therefore, the chief instrument which we employ in such
studies, for these disciplines can be understood and
enjoyed only by mental processes of the same type as
created them. We follow again the path taken by
someone's thinking and under his guidance. To do this
to the best advantage we should have some understanding of what thinking involves.

Thought is the response that we make to a problem.
There are two kinds of situations which we have to deal
with—situations for which we have an answer ready and
situations which are new to us. In the first case the

---

*Op. cit.
†J. S. Mill—*A System of Logic*, Introduction, § 5.

answer may be one which is provided in our inherited make-up, it may be one which we have discovered for ourselves, or it may be one which we have learned from someone else. In the second case such dependence on " what we did the last time " will not help us. We must invent or discover a suitable course of action.

Such a discovery may be made by trial and error. Not knowing what to do, we do something at random and hope for the best. This is the method of the cat or the dog in the puzzle-box (p. 49)—the most primitive way of dealing with a novel situation. The characteristically human way is to seek an answer to the problem by reflective thought. The power to do this distinguishes man from the beasts and makes him a rational animal, *homo sapiens*.

The problem may be a practical one—to uncork a bottle without a corkscrew, to restart the engine of a car which has come to a standstill, to invent a piece of mechanism, to cure or prevent a disease, to devise a better economic or political system, to induce someone to adopt a course of action which we think desirable. It may be purely theoretical—to square the circle, to account for the occurrence of sea-shells in geological strata far above sea-level, to harmonize the Christian tradition with the philosophy of Aristotle, to throw light upon the mysteries of human experience, to consider the meaning of pain and " justifie the wayes of God to men." Whether our reason is employed upon some trifling and temporary difficulty or upon some metaphysical problem, its processes are essentially the same. Thus, the interest with which we follow an argument in scholarship or science, in philology or mathematics, in history or physics, is at least in part similar to that with which we follow a detective story. The work of the scientist and the philosopher may to this extent be described as detection without crime.

What is happening when we think ? In other words, what was taking place in the mind of Sherlock Holmes while he was smoking his three pipes ? Thinking begins when we find ourselves face to face with a problem. Apart from a problem and our awareness of it, we cannot begin to think at all. Once we begin to think about a problem, it may be difficult to stop : there is an insistant desire to know the answer. It is from this desire that human knowledge comes, including all the subject matter of the learner's studies. Every fact or theory which he may have to master was once at least the object of someone's curiosity. It is therefore potentially interesting. There are in fact no dull subjects of study, though there may be dull students—or dull teachers or writers. Apart from that curiosity, the fact or theory would never have been discovered or set forth. Apart from a similar curiosity, it cannot be profitably studied. Thus here also interest is of primary importance. The first step in any new study is the awakening of the interest to which it is the answer. If a subject seems dull to a student, it is because he is not approaching it with the right interest or with the knowledge which is necessary in order to grasp what he is reading about.

The second step in thinking is to examine the problem with which we have to deal in order to see it clearly. We must *stop* and think. There is therefore a cessation of outward activity. The school accustoms us to problems in arithmetic and other departments of mathematics in which this part of our thinking is done for us. The essentials of the problem are stated without ambiguity, omission or superfluity. Even then the nature of the problem may be mistaken, if it is not read with sufficient care. Nothing is commoner in reading examination scripts than to find that the examinee, instead of answering the question set him, is answering another for which he has mistaken it, no doubt a far better and more convenient one. This may have been deliberate, as in the story of the theological student who met a request for the names of the major and minor prophets with the tactful reply: " Far be it from me to make invidious distinctions between these holy men. I shall therefore give instead a list of the Kings of Israel," a subject with which he was doubtless better prepared. In most cases it means that the examinee has read the question paper with insufficient care.

However this may be, the text-book or examination question does not prepare us for the very real difficulty of correctly locating and formulating for ourselves a problem of real life, and it leaves us unprotected against such catch questions as the familiar :

If one train leaves London at 10 a.m. travelling at 40 miles per hour, and another leaves Edinburgh at 10.30 travelling at 35 miles an hour, but stopping at Berwick for 40 minutes and at Newcastle for 45 minutes, which will be nearer to London when they meet ?

or even :

Which will pass the other first ?

Most of the facts given here are irrelevant, but, while we are trying to assemble them all in our minds, we miss the absurdity of the question and the absence of the essential fact, are the trains travelling to Edinburgh and London respectively, or is the first train perhaps bound for Exeter ? If we first note the exact nature of the problem to which we want an answer, we can then examine the facts which we are given in order to see which of them are relevant to it and in what way.

When a problem is not presented to us in words, examining it means using our powers of observation. Perception is the servant of observation. It would have little value if the impressions of our senses were received in our minds as passively as impressions of light and shadow are received on a photographic plate. Observation is an active process, and depends not only on what we see or hear, but on our ability to interpret, and on the purpose which we have in view in making our observations. Dr. Watson, in the adventure of " The Blue Carbuncle,"* can study the battered billycock through Sherlock Holmes's lens (" You know my methods. Apply them.") and observe its colour, its shape, the signs of wear, the colour of the lining, the stains, the initials, the pierced brim, the missing elastic, the dust, the spots, and the attempt to hide them with ink.

" I can see nothing," said I, handing it back to my friend.
" On the contrary, Watson, you can see everything. You fail, however, to reason from what you see.   You are too timid in drawing your inferences."

Holmes then proceeds to read what is written on the hat—that its owner was highly intellectual, that he was fairly well-to-do within the last three years, though now fallen on evil days, that he leads a sedentary life, that he is middle-aged, that he has grizzled hair, that he has had it cut recently, that it is improbable that he has gas laid on in his house, that he has now less foresight than he had formerly, indicating some evil influence, probably drink, which would account for the fact that his wife has ceased to love him.

This arrests the attention. It is meant to do so. Yet there is nothing here (apart from the atmosphere of parody) that is not a commonplace of scientific method. We may compare with it the words of Dr. Joseph Bell, one of Conan Doyle's teachers, when he was a student

---

*Conan Doyle—*The Adventures of Sherlock Holmes.*

of medicine at Edinburgh, and the reputed model for Sherlock Holmes :

> Eyes and ears which can see and hear, memory to record at once and to recall at pleasure the impression of the senses, and an imagination capable of weaving a theory or piecing together a broken chain or unravelling a tangled clue, such are the implements of his trade to a successful diagnostician.*

Here are the remarks of Charles Darwin on the subject. Writing of someone who said that he (Darwin) should have published only the facts which he had discovered, he says :†

> How profoundly ignorant [he] must be of the very soul of observation ! About thirty years ago there was much talk that geologists ought only to observe, and not theorize : and I well remember someone saying that at this rate a man might as well go into a gravel pit and count the pebbles, and describe the colours. How odd it is that anyone should not see that all observation must be for or against some view if it is to be of any service.

In exactly the same spirit Holmes, in the story of " Silver Blaze,"‡ digs out of the mud into which it has been trampled the half-burned wax vesta which is the vital clue.

> " I cannot think how I came to overlook it," said the Inspector, with an expression of annoyance.
> " It was invisible, buried in the mud. I only saw it because I was looking for it."

His observation is made in the light of a theory already formed and in order to test it.

---

*Q. in Hesketh Pearson—*Op. cit.*, p. 89.
†Leslie Stephen—*Life of Henry Fawcett*, p. 100.
‡Conan Doyle—*The Memoirs of Sherlock Holmes.*

The third stage in dealing with a problem is to bring to bear upon it the facts or principles necessary for its solution. We may not be acquainted with them. If so we can make no progress until we have obtained such an acquaintance. Why did Sir John Franklin's expedition in search of the North-West passage fail so miserably ? It consisted of carefully chosen personnel. It was well equipped. There was plenty of food. In recent years we have learned that vitamin C is necessary to life, that the lime-juice carried by the Franklin expedition as a precaution against scurvy (the disease due to lack of this vitamin) would contain little of it after being kept for two years, that the fresh food obtained by hunting was cooked in a way to destroy its vitamin C content, that the lassitude and depression from which they suffered resembled symptons of vitamin C deficiency. Thus Stefansson can put forward scurvy as the explanation with confidence. Without our present knowledge it could not have been suggested, and without that knowledge the commander of the expedition was unable to prevent disaster, though the means of doing so were to hand in the everyday diet of the Esquimaux beside him, which the prejudice of white men against primitive habits no doubt prevented him from even considering.*

This third stage is very like the " happy moment " in which nerves and muscles suddenly get the knack of a new movement. Just because the movement is new to us it cannot be made as a result of a direct effort of will and such efforts, since they can direct our nervous energy only into established channels, militate against its occurrence. Similarly here, since the idea or principle which we require, is not one which we are accustomed to apply in this connection—if it were, there would be no need to stop and think—we cannot summon it up at will.

---

*Vilhjalmur Stefansson—*Unsolved Mysteries of the Arctic.*

What is required is rather a certain passivity or openness of mind, a waiting attitude. Nothing may happen. Or—if we are fortunate—the required idea may appear shyly, like a diffident stranger, uncertain of his reception, on the fringes of the mind. It is necessary to learn to be on the look-out for such appearances, to be aware that at first sight they may seem, like most new ideas, somewhat bizarre or futile, and to note them for careful examination. Otherwise they are easily lost, and the mind returns to its well-trodden round of familiar but unhelpful ideas.

We may possess the knowledge necessary to solve a problem and yet fail because we do not bring it to mind. Here is a little detective story. In the days of flint-lock guns a man returned home from shooting on a summer day and was found later lying on a sofa shot through the heart. His gun, which lay on a table by the window beside a large bible and a bowl of gold fish, had been discharged, though the trigger had not been pulled. He could not have shot himself and then laid the gun on the table, for death must have been immediate. No one else could have entered the room. Was it murder, accident or suicide ? The answer depends upon one small item of everyday knowledge. You may possess it, but you may not think of it in connection with the problem. If you do, the answer will at once be clear.* This is often the critical stage in thinking. Thus a rider in geometry may be solved as soon as we see that it is a case of angles in a semi-circle which must be right-angles and therefore equal, or equiangular triangles, the sides of which must be in the same ratio.

What can we do to facilitate the occurrence of such an idea ? It is partly a matter of association. Some aspect of the problem as we have stated it to ourselves is

*The answer will be found at the end of the Chapter.

linked to the fact or principle which we require in order
to solve it. In the example taken, it was the bowl of
gold fish. As we turn the problem over in our minds,
we give its factors the opportunity to bring this fact or
principle to mind. When it comes, we call it a " brain
wave," an " inspiration " or a " bright idea," as if it
were independent of our efforts, and came to us from
outside bringing with it a sudden illumination. Sometimes, just because our conscious efforts are on the wrong
track, and are preventing instead of facilitating its
occurrence, it may be well to put the problem out of the
mind, to think about something else, to " sleep on it "—
and by and by the desired answer may present itself
unasked. The essential thinking has been done for us
by mental processes not under our control or within our
observations.

We may deliberately avail ourselves of such processes.
Thus in an examination a candidate may have four
questions to answer. Let him begin by reading through
the paper carefully, choosing the four questions most
suitable and noting the main points that he can make in
answer to each. Five minutes spent on this before he
begins to write at all may be the most profitable five
minutes of the time allowed to him. Let him then
embark on the question he thinks he can answer best.
While he is at work upon it, answers to the other three
will be forming in his mind and, when he comes to them,
he will be surprised to find how much he knows about
them and how quickly he can put it on paper. Confidence
in these subconscious processes will facilitate their
occurrence. To get flustered will hinder them. Emotion
narrows the mind and limits the range of its activity.

A second precaution that we can take is to make sure
that we are giving due consideration to all the terms of
the problem. In doing a crossword puzzle we may know

the number of letters that a word contains, one or two of the letters and their position in the word, and we may have some hint as to its meaning. These facts limit the number of possible answers. To lose sight of any one of them is to receive and entertain unsuitable suggestions. It may be difficult to keep them all in view at once. Lady Abbott,* a " dumb blonde," wanted the name of an Italian composer in nine letters beginning with P. Her " span of apprehension " being too narrow to contain so many items at once, she vainly tried—and rejected—*Irving Berlin*, who had too many letters, *Puccini*, who had too few, and *Mussolini*, who was not a composer, according as one or other of the requirements was uppermost in her mind. When Sir Buckstone triumphantly wrote in *Pagliacci* for her, one of them was still imperfectly satisfied.

The fourth stage in thinking is the critical examination of the suggestion which has come to us at stage three. There are two tests that we can apply : First, does it satisfy all the conditions laid down at stage one ? and, secondly, what consequences must follow if it is true, and can we, by observation or experiment, discover whether such consequences do in fact follow ? In some cases we need only see that the conditions of the problem are satisfied. What odd two-figure number is the cube of a single-figure number ? The only single-figure numbers whose cubes lie between 10 and 99 are 3 and 4, and, since the answer cannot be an even number, any multiple of which must be an even number, we are left with 3, the cube of which is 27. It is otherwise with Lady Abbott's question. Further research might have led her to consider *Pergolesi*, who was an Italian and a composer and had nine letters in his name. But this is not the end of the matter, for there may be other Italian

* P. G. Wodehouse—*Summer Moonshine*, Chapt. XXI.

composers who satisfy these conditions equally well. If, however, we put the matter to the test by writing the name in, we can see whether it affords a clue to some of the words which cross it. If it does, that is good evidence that it is the right name, even if someone now suggests *Paisiello*.

In the natural sciences it is more often necessary to test the suggestion in this second way—by inferring what must follow if it is true and going back to nature to see whether the facts of the case agree with our inferences. The suggestion is in fact what the scientist calls a *hypothesis*—a provisional theory which accounts for the facts which we know. We can therefore say of it that it is true as far as we know, and we can use it as a starting point for further inquiry by which it may be proved or disproved. Thus we may ask why iron rusts and suggest, as the result of everyday experience, that the presence of moisture has something to do with it. That is our hypothesis. If this is the true explanation, there can be no rusting where there is no moisture. That is an inference from the hypothesis, and it is one which we can test. We can take some bright, new, iron nails and seal them up in a bottle which has been carefully dried. If rusting takes place, that will disprove our hypothesis. If no rusting takes place, that will support our hypothesis. It will not prove it to be the true explanation, for, when we sealed the bottle up, we may have excluded some other factor, which is the essential one. This consideration may suggest another experiment —sealing the nails up as before but with some distilled water. If they rust this time we have come very near to confirmation of our hypothesis, so far as it asserts water to be one factor necessary. To find whether it is the only one, we may repeat the experiment, this time filling the bottle with water which we know to have neither solids nor gases dissolved in it. If on this occasion there is no rusting, we may conclude that the presence of moisture is not the only condition necessary, and therefore that our hypothesis is not the whole explanation. We must then modify the hypothesis, let us say by supposing the presence of air to be a second necessary factor, and devise an experiment to test this suggestion.

Scientific knowledge, and perhaps most of our knowledge, is of this kind. It consists of theories, provisional hypotheses, which have so far stood the tests to which we have put them. They are true as far as we know, and so we continue to treat them as true, until we find a case in which they break down. That will be an opportunity for framing a new theory to cover this new case, and for further observation and experiment to test it. This is the method of science, and also the method which we follow in practical life.

Very often a problem is easily solved if we can so arrange its terms that their relationships to one another are easily understood. There is a moment of " insight " and the necessary mental operations then seem to take place almost of themselves. There is an ancient problem which has caused much heated argument and much distress of mind. A speaker standing before a portrait is supposed to say :

> Sisters and brothers have I none,
> But that man's father is my father's son.

What is the relationship of the speaker to the man in the picture ? Part of the difficulty is in the jingle. Part of it is in the three points of reference, " I," " that man " and " my father." We try to unravel this tangle from each of these points in turn and give up and try another. Part of it is in the arrangement ; for the key to the problem, the real starting point, is in the last phrase. Who is " my father's son " ? " I " am my father's son and, if I have no brothers, my father's only son. We can now omit the first line, change " my father's son " into " I " and write the second line in this form :

That man's father is I.

which means

I am that man's father.

that is

That man is my son.

When we " turn over a problem " in our minds we are engaged in arranging and re-arranging its terms until they fall into a pattern in which some vital relationship between them is made more evident. The mind is quick to seize upon such a relationship and to proceed from it to some further conception which is implied. MAN *is to* WOMAN *as* BOY *is to* ? The first two words indicate the relationship of male and female. The word to be supplied must bear this relationship to the word BOY. But the reader's mind has already supplied it without the need to go through this piece of reasoning. NORTH *is to* SOUTH *as* EAST *is to* ? This time the relationship is that of opposite points of the compass. GOOD *is to* BAD *as* THICK *is to* ? 6 *is to* 3 *as* 10 *is to* ? CIRCLE *is to* SPHERE *as* SQUARE *is to* ? In each case we have two terms which at once suggest some familiar relationship which exists between them, and we use that relationship as a bridge to carry us from the third term to a new one which stands in the desired relationship to it.

Sometimes our thinking must set out from one term and a relationship which is named : Which is the figure which has one more side than a triangle ? What is the masculine of *daughter* ? What is the opposite of *benevolent* ? What is six times seven, or the square of four, or the cube root of twenty-seven ? Who is the head of the executive in a monarchy, in a republic ? Sometimes the terms are given and the relationship has to be found : What is the relationship of six to nine ? Of dark to light ? Of fear to terror ? Of timidity to fear ? Of water to rust ? Of food rationing to national standards of nutrition ? Of unemployment to political instability ? Of a general rise in wages to a subsequent fall in the purchasing power of money ?

It has been claimed,* after lengthy experimental study, that all our thinking proceeds in one or other of these ways from what is " given "—that is, from what is supplied by perception, or by the man who sets the problem—to what is supplied by the mind, from the evidence to the theory, from the clue to the criminal. There are therefore two directions in which we can develop our powers of thinking. We can increase the number of the relationshipsthat we are able to recognise, and we can increase our facility in applying these relationships to bridge the gap between something we have got and something we wish to discover. This rather than acquiring information or amassing facts is the aim of our studies.

Our perception of relationships may be as immediate as our perception of objects themselves. When the reader looks at Fig. 13 he perceives two squares but he cannot be aware of them without also being aware of some of the relationships in which they stand to one another. Thus they are side by side. One is larger than the other. The larger is on the right of the smaller. The smaller is to the left of the larger. They are alike in having their sides parallel to the sides of the page.

Those relationships are familiar to us. We first met them so long ago that we have no recollection of ever

---

* C. Spearman—*The Nature of " Intelligence " and the Principles of Cognition* 1923.

having learned them, and we have met them many times since. They are part of the mental furniture which we bring with us to the perception of objects. There is here something very similar to the mental processes made evident in the experiment with Fig. 7. In that case the mind imposed upon the objects a series of patterns for which there was no justification in the objects themselves, yet these patterns appeared to present themselves to our attention without our making any effort to find them. Here, in much the same way, as we look at a group of objects, or the factors of a problem,

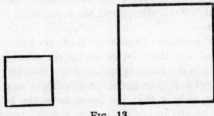

FIG. 13.

we grasp them in terms of relationships with which we are familiar—relative position, relative size, similarity, difference, cause and effect, opposite, incompatible and so on.

The particular relationship to which we give our attention in any particular case will depend upon the purpose which we have in view. Thus if the two squares are in fact pieces of cake, the relationship relevant to the action which we are to decide upon is that of size : the one on the left is smaller and so good manners require that we select it. Or it may be that of position : always help yourself to the piece that is nearest to you.

It must also be noted that the relationships which we see may not exhaust the possibilities of a situation. In the case of the squares in Fig. 13 there are other relationships which are not so evident. Thus it is necessary to measure the squares to be sure that the sides of the one are twice as long as the sides of the other, and that the distance between them is equal to the length of the diagonal of the smaller square. When these relationships are known, it may then be evident that the area of the smaller square is one-fourth of the area of the larger, that the distance between them is equal to half the length of the diagonal of the larger square or the length of one of its sides divided by $\sqrt{2}$, or these further relationships may not be evident. It depends upon what mental equipment we bring with us to the perception.

We are applying knowledge that we have learned. To a school boy the relative size of the areas may still be a matter for profound and painful thought. To the mathematician it is as immediately evident as that they are side by side or that the larger is on the left. This difference results in the main from the difference in the number of times that they have made use of this relationship in thinking about questions of area. The two further relationships mentioned are also dependent upon the seeing of relationships familiar from previous experience of them, in the study or application of mathematics. They depend upon the equality of things which are equal to the same thing, the relation between the hypotenuse of a right-angled triangle and the other two sides, the constancy of the relations between the lengths of the sides in a series of triangles of different size but with their corresponding angles equal. Again the school boy may need to state these principles laboriously to himself because of their relative unfamiliarity to him.

To commit such principles to memory is not very helpful. What we want is not the power of repeating to ourselves a certain formula—a gramophone record could do that—but the power of applying the principle as a tool for thinking with. The best way to learn to do this is to use it over and over again. If we have this practical kind of familiarity with it, we shall not find much difficulty in putting it into words when we want to do so. This will happen if we want to explain it to someone else, or if we want to discuss it, in order to inquire whether it is true, or how far it is true. But in these cases also mere getting it by heart is not a good substitute for understanding it or for ready skill in putting it to use.

There are some students who say that they must learn such things by heart as a means to understanding them. They would do well to consider whether this is not merely a bad habit which has resulted from wrong methods of learning in early school-days. Learning then meant for them learning by heart ; a grasp of the meaning came, if at all, after the thing was learned, and, never having become acquainted with more efficient mental habits, they have continued to learn in this fashion.

Sometimes such methods are actually encouraged in school. They represent a very old tradition, for in the days before printing, and still more in the days before the general use of writing, schooling meant memorising the actual words of the work being studied. Some pupils still attempt to do this with *Euclid,* and an eminent scholar has recently confessed in an autobiography that he never used any other method. He also, which is not surprising, found the subject unprofitable. It is as unprofitable as learning by heart a series of jokes of which one does not see the point. If one sees the point of a joke, one may in re-telling it give it " a new hat and stick " every time and yet it may still be the same joke. If one does not see the point of it, one can only seek for verbal accuracy on the basis of mechanical memory, and, with some little change of which we are unaware, the point goes altogether.

In some cases to understand, or think that one understands, the relationship between the factors of a problem is to be ready to take the next step. In other cases the next step may not be quite so clear. Six is two-thirds of nine. The presence of moisture is a necessary condition of rusting. A timid person is one who is liable to experience fear, when a less timid person would not. When many persons are unemployed, their thoughts naturally go to remedies of a political kind and their numbers give them weight. We can see in these cases what the connection is.

In other cases it may require investigation. Thus statistics show that rationing may result in an improvement in nutrition even in circumstances of scarcity. In some cases it may be difficult to find an answer. Is terror a more intense degree of fear or does a further element, a breaking down of normal self-control enter into it ? In other cases we may see that many factors and other relationships must be considered. Thus a rise in wages may bring more efficient production. At the same time it may lead to an increased demand, since people have more money to spend. Production will in consequence be on a larger scale, and this may mean a decrease in production costs and therefore a rise in the purchasing power of money at home and a favourable position in foreign markets with the consequent opportunity of buying more goods abroad. What applies in one industry may not apply in another. Thus it might prove that the manufacture of refrigerators in larger quantities would make possible a reduction in price, whereas this advantage may already have been fully exploited in some other class of goods, say bicycles or sewing-machines ; while in another case, let us say that of coal or wheat, the cost of production may actually go up with an increase in production, because less accessible seams must be worked or less fertile land cultivated. Again, this may be offset by better methods, for example, the use of machinery or improved methods of cultivation. Thus what may seem at first a simple relationship may prove on examination to be a complex system of many inter-related factors.

Murder, accident or suicide ?

The relevant piece of knowledge is the properties of a burning glass. The gold-fish bowl acted in this way, focussing the rays of the sun on the flashpan of the gun and discharging it.

NOTE

There is a mistake in the upper part of Fig. 1. If the reader turned to it as an illustration of the account of reflex action given in the text, he may have seen nothing wrong. If he will now turn to p. 16 and ask himself what is wrong with the picture, he will easily find the error. The purpose with which we examine something helps to determine what we notice (*see* pp. 93–6).

Part III
THE CONDUCT OF THE MIND

CHAPTER VIII

CALM OF MIND

> . . . they who feel Shame grow red, and they who
> fear Death turn pale. So both are evidently in a way
> physical. . . .

> . . . wee understood
> Her by her sight ; her pure, and eloquent blood
> Spoke in her cheekes, and so distinctly wrought,
> That one might almost say, her body thought ; . . .

> Certainly I must confess my own barbarousness, I have
> never heard the old song of Percy and Douglas, that I
> found not my heart moved more than with a trumpet.

It is difficult to explain in words what an emotion is,
but it is easy to name some of the emotions. Fear,
anger, disgust, elation and dejection are familiar examples. Though difficult to describe, an emotion is easy
to recognise when it is experienced. There is nothing
contradictory in this, and the same is true of other
experiences. Thus it is impossible to describe a smell,
and it would be quite impossible to describe a colour to
a blind man who had never had the use of his eyes,
though we easily recognise smells or colours and name
them.

We can indicate in general terms what an emotion
feels like. It involves some degree of mental unrest or
excitement, accompanied by some perturbation of body.
It is likely to be distinctly pleasant or unpleasant, and

Note.—The quotations at the head of the chapter are from : Aristotle—*Ethics*,
IV, xi, tr. Chase ; John Donne—*Complete Poetry and Selected Prose*, ed. Hayward,
" The Second Anniversary," *ll.* 243-6 ; Sir Philip Sidney—*The Defence of Poesy*.

the same emotion may be pleasant on one occasion and unpleasant on another. Thus fear may be pleasant when it takes the form of the " thrills " which we seek in slightly dangerous sports. It is perhaps the most horrible experience we can have, when it is intense, as in a nightmare.

Emotions are closely linked to wanting or desiring. To be afraid is to be aware of some danger, real or imaginary, and to have an impulse to withdraw from it, and the fear is likely to be intense in proportion to the seriousness of the anticipated danger and the difficulty of withdrawing in safety. We are aware of a certain tenseness in the situation, a tenseness which is really within ourselves. This feeling of strain comes from the rising impulse to withdraw and something which prevents us from yielding to it, such as our knowledge that the way of escape is blocked or that duty requires us to stand fast. If the danger passes, or if we face it and deal with it, the tension is relieved, and the perturbation subsides, though not perhaps at once.

The other emotions are also accompanied by impulses. Thus anger goes with an impulse to attack and destroy or drive away the person or thing that obstructs us. Wonder accompanies an impulse to gaze admiringly, disgust an impulse to spit out or push away the disgusting object, elation an impulse to exhibit ourselves to the admiration and congratulations of others, dejection the impulse to shrink from notice.

Emotion is accompanied by changes in the body. Some of these changes can be readily observed by another person—the expression of the face, the posture of the body, the tone of voice, tears or laughter, threat or entreaty, an attitude of triumph or despair.

Emotion is accompanied by other bodily changes which are not so easily observed. Such are accelerated or retarded breathing, a quicker heartbeat, a drying up of the mouth. There are also changes which can be detected only by the use of suitable apparatus in the laboratory. Thus the electrical resistance of the body alters in conditions of emotional excitement. This is shown by an instrument which records the resistance of the hand to an electrical current, alterations in the resistance being shown by the movement of a little spot-light on a screen. The subject is stimulated in ways likely to arouse slight momentary emotional responses and these are found to be accompanied by movements of the light.

The chemical condition of the body is also altered when emotion is experienced, for emotion is accompanied by changes in the rate of activity of the various glands. Sorrow leads to increased activity of the tear glands— and we weep. The smell of food when we are hungry arouses an increased activity of the salivary glands— the mouth waters. Fear on the other hand decreases their activity and the mouth goes dry so that speech may be difficult. Fear also decreases the digestive secretions and so arrests the processes of digestion. Of equal or perhaps greater importance are chemical changes which escape our attention and which have been discovered only in recent times. Some of these are due to activities of the *endocrine glands*, which pass their secretions directly into the blood. They produce effects upon the body much in the same way that drugs do, when introduced into the blood artificially. A striking case is that of the small glands, one on the top of each kidney, called the *adrenal glands*. The substance they secrete is passed into the blood in larger amounts in conditions of excitement, involving fear or anger. This results in a decrease in the amount of blood circulating in the digestive organs and an increase in the amount of

blood in the muscles, with a consequent retardation
of digestion and increase in available muscular energy.
There is also an increase in the coagulability of the blood,
so that its power of solidifying on exposure to the air,
so as to seal up a small wound and prevent further
bleeding, is improved.

These bodily changes which accompany emotions
take place without the intervention of the will, being
brought about by reflex action. Sometimes they take
place in spite of our efforts to prevent them, as in the
case of blushing. We feel ourselves growing redder
almost in proportion as we wish to arrest these tell-tale
signs.

To a great extent the bodily changes accompanying
emotions are useful changes. If you meet a sudden
danger and must run for your life, a deep breath—the
gasp of fear—is the first useful step to running away.
If you are obstructed by someone and get red in the face
and shout at him, you may frighten him off. If you are
going to run away or to fight, digestion can wait, and
you want an ample supply of blood in your muscles, so
that you may be capable of the utmost exertion. Also,
in such a situation, you may be wounded, and a greater
adrenalin secretion with greater coagulability of the
blood may save your life.

In the civilised world we are less often exposed to the
need for sudden flight or a fight for life, and so these once
useful responses are less often appropriate. If we lose
our tempers and shout and stamp our feet, we are more
likely to be despised as " childish " than to make a
favourable impression. They have a further disadvantage. Not only do they make an alteration in the whole
bodily economy, but once this alteration is made, it
takes some time for the chemical changes to pass away
and so the emotion takes some time to subside. If I say

" Next Tuesday is the 15th," and then correct myself and say " No, it is the 16th," I have wasted some breath and a few seconds of time, but that is all. If, through a misunderstanding I become angry, and then have my mistake pointed out to me, my anger does not stop because I have perceived that it is unwarranted. No doubt I apologise, and on the surface the error seems to be corrected, but if my glandular activities have been affected, the results in my body persist for an hour or two, and during that period I am more likely to be irritable and easily provoked than if the first flash of temper had not occurred, and I am less fit for mental work.

Even when the emotional perturbation has passed and the body has returned to normal, the fact that the emotion has occurred may influence later experiences. This happens through a kind of learning which takes place without any awareness on our part. When any person or object has aroused an emotion in us we are liable to feel the same emotion again whenever we see or think about that person or object. The person or object for which we have once felt the emotion is now a stimulus which sets off the reflexes which control the bodily part of it and so it floods our minds. Thus we approach with fear a person who has once frightened us, we are on the alert and ready for the offensive in the presence of some-one who has once angered us, we feel disgust at the thought of someone who has behaved meanly, and we sit ready to admire or ready to laugh before someone who has previously excited our admiration or our laughter.

An emotion is something in us, an unusual condition of our minds and bodies. Sometimes we do not recognise this. The angry man believes he is the only person present who is quite cool and collected, and he will assure you quite sincerely that this is the case. The young man in love does not consider himself in an irrational frame of mind which blinds his judgment : he marvels at the blindness of the rest of the world to the pre-eminent beauty and angelic virtues of his sweetheart :—

> Nay, but you who do not love her,
>   Is she not pure gold, my mistress ?
> Holds earth ought, speak truth, above her ? . . .

This is not quite what her sister, her quite normally affectionate and appreciative sister, thinks of her, but then her sister is in a less emotional state of mind. When Viola and Sir Andrew Aguecheek tremble before one another, it is because each seems to the other a terrible man of war and each is too terrified to notice the other's pallor or knocking knees. Under the influence of an emotion, we attribute to the object, which arouses it, qualities which it may not in fact possess, qualities which would justify the emotion which we are experiencing. The world appears a place of gloom to the man whose liver is out of order, a cheerful place to someone more eupeptic. The same object may be quite differently perceived according to the emotion experienced in its presence—a point wittily illustrated in the *Punch* drawings reproduced in Fig. 14.

Emotion has another characteristic which must be noted. It results in a narrowing of consciousness. To be afraid, to be anxious, is to be unable to turn our thoughts from the object of our fear or anxiety. Become angry at someone's word or action, and it occupies the attention to the exclusion of everything else. His good qualities, his kindness or help on other occasions are forgotten, for the recollection of them is incompatible with the anger of which he is at present the object. Damocles, we may be sure, could give little attention

Miss White as seen by Mr. Averageman

Miss White as seen by little Willie Green

Miss White as seen by Miss Black

Miss White as seen by Mr. Brown about to visit his dentist

Reproduced by permission of the Proprietors of PUNCH

FIG. 14.

to the food and wine before him, or to his host's conversation, while the sword hung by a single hair over his head.

These three characteristics of emotion are of great importance in relation to study. Learning means trying to do new things, things we have still to master, things which we do with difficulty or fail to do altogether. It is therefore easy to be discouraged, to feel annoyed, to become afraid or anxious about our success. Next time we come to the task, we come with an attitude involving these emotions. We therefore come unwillingly. Our energy, instead of going freely and easily into the activities of learning, is being used up in conflict with this negative attitude. Our progress is therefore less than it would otherwise be. We blame this, not on our own fears and anxieties, but on the difficulty of the task, and as this attitude to it becomes more strongly established, the task does become *for us* an insuperable one—but a great part of the difficulty is in ourselves, not in the task, and it is difficult to recognise that this is so. We cannot approach the task without this attitude to it, and so, on each occasion, mind and body are in an unfavourable condition for learning. In particular the narrowing of consciousness which is a consequence of any such emotion robs us of the fertility and vivacity of mind which are essential.

The reader may have noticed, but failed to understand, an experience so common that every student seems to recognise it when described to him. A certain chapter is prescribed for an examination. You sit down conscientiously to read it, with a determination to impress its contents firmly upon your mind. Having read the first paragraph, or the first page, you recall your wandering thoughts, ask yourself how much of it you have understood or memorized, and begin again at the beginning. This time you get a little further before doubts again assail you and you turn back. The more effort you make the less you seem to grasp, and presently your mind wanders and the book is allowed to close. Perhaps as you pick it up again your eye is caught by something in another chapter. You begin to read with interest, until you suddenly remind yourself that this is not what you ought to be doing, and you turn wearily to the passage which has been set. Why is the set passage so dull and difficult ? Because it has been deliberately chosen for these qualities ? This is very unlikely. Its apparent dullness is due to the spirit in which you have approached it, weighed down with a feeling of responsibility, saying, " I must understand, I must remember," fearing that you will neither understand nor remember, and accordingly not in a fit state of mind to do either. When you read the other chapter, you gave the author a chance. Your mind was free to receive and play about his ideas. In other words you were interested, and therefore you understood, and since you understood, there was no question of making an effort to remember. We might almost lay down a rule : Never try to remember what you read. Always try to understand what you read. Memorise afterwards, if necessary.

Nothing is in itself easy or difficult. It is easy or difficult in relation to somebody who is attempting it, and what is difficult for one person is easy for another. The learner's task is always difficult, for he is attempting something that has not yet been made easy by practice and familiarity. In so far as he is successful and feels himself to be getting on, he experiences elation, and this is favourable to his further progress. In so far as he is unsuccessful, or, what comes to the same thing, unaware of such success as he is meeting with, he becomes discouraged, bored, anxious, less able to profit by the efforts he is making, and less and less willing to make them. He may express his dissatisfaction by saying that his task is difficult, forgetting how many things he now does with ease that once caused him pain and trouble. Or he may call himself a fool and declare that he is no good at this, forgetting that we are all fools at the things we have not yet learned to do.

From such situations an attitude may develop which forms a permanent obstacle to a particular line of study. It is an unnecessary obstacle, and one which may conceal the fact that the mental powers and potential interest required for success are there. It may be partly met by considering the progress that has actually been made in the subject, instead of dwelling only on the " undone vast " still to be attacked. It can be met by action : do not sit looking at the bit you can't do, but do the bit you can. The remainder will then look less formidable, and perhaps it may prove to have been outflanked altogether. In other cases the explanation may be that the difficulty has been attacked in the wrong way. What is wanted is a new technique of learning, or perhaps a different text-book. Or some necessary step may have been missed and all that is needed is to go back and pick up the dropped stitch—the term or principle which has not been grasped, the technical device which has not been sufficiently mastered. In other cases there may be two difficulties which seem insuperable together, but which may be easily overcome by tackling them separately, as a child at school who is poor at essay writing may be helped by giving separate attention for a time to writing, spelling and oral composition, the combined difficulty of constructing sentences, spelling out the words and producing a clean and legible script being at the moment too much for him.

The most favourable state of mind for study seems to be one in which we try our best, are rewarded with some success, and feel as a result sufficient confidence to try again. A good teacher will keep his pupil in this favourable state of mind by giving judicious encouragement when it is needed. The private student will do well to cultivate a similar attitude by noting his own progress. Unfortunately the occasions upon which such encouragement would be most valuable are those in which there are fewest indications of progress to justify it. The student cannot disguise this situation from himself as a teacher would disguise it from him by a little praise based upon faith rather than works. He can, however, discount the unfavourable effects of discouragement by deliberately reminding himself that such feelings make a difficulty seem greater than it really is, that some ebb and flow of feeling is as natural to study as to any other activity, and that a corresponding feeling of triumph will follow when success is achieved.

On the whole an equable state of mind is more favourable to intellectual achievement than violent fluctuations of feeling. This does not mean that study is a dull business. The uphill, plodding toil of mastering new material may be rewarded by a sudden vision as exciting as Cortez's first view of the Pacific. We may recall in this connection the student of Euclid who exclaimed delightedly, " Now I know what an argument is. Now I know when something is proved." Or Archimedes rushing triumphantly from the public baths shouting, " Eureka ! " (I have found it !) when the solution of his problem occurred to him.

It is also as well to be aware of the possibility of cultivating an intellectual interest. Just as we desire to return to a place where we have been happy, so we have a ready inclination to return to any activity of mind or body which we have enjoyed. The elation felt at success in intellectual work is as real as the elation felt at any other kind of success. An intellectual interest, like an interest in a game or a hobby, grows out of a succession of occasions upon which we have experienced such pleasurable feelings. The strength of such an interest will carry us through many later discouraging difficulties or much dull plodding that must precede the next achievement.

The study of poetry, painting or music is related to the emotions in a special way which must be noted here. In the arts emotion is part of the subject matter under consideration. There would be little profit in studying a joke if one did not see the point of it and feel it to be funny, or in reading a tragedy if one was not moved by the tragic emotions of pity and terror. Works of art ask of us something more than a purely intellectual response.

A work of art is a unity in a sense that does not apply to a work of science or philosophy. " The thoughts even of a lyrical poem do not follow one another at haphazard . . . the links [are] forged by feeling rather than by logic, yet the feelings must be such as can be traced, and the mind cannot be really in sympathy with the poem unless consciously or unconsciously it follows them."* One of the aims in studying a poem is therefore to trace these links. This each of us must do for himself, and the first step is so to read the poem as to be moved by it. No two readers will be moved in exactly the same way.† The comments of another may therefore seem to him " superfluous, if not prosaic and inadequate."‡

---

* E. C. Wickham—*Quinti Horatii Opera Omnia*, Vol I, Preface.
† Readers may even differ as to whether a character is to be regarded sympathetically or as a laughing stock. Falstaff and Malvolio are instances. F. A. Wright, in *Three Roman Poets* (1938, pp. 197-8) indicates three entirely diverse attitudes to Ovid's *Ars Amatoria*.
‡ Wickham—*ibid.*

Thus Bentley was for Pope the

> . . . mighty Scholiast, whose unweary'd pains
> Made Horace dull, and humbled Milton's strains.*

Pope had his own reasons for jibing at Bentley and a
critic's comments may help the reader to a deeper understanding than he can reach for himself, an understanding
in which he does not need to admit, on account of defects
in his knowledge, "the existence of ' inert ' epithets and
purposeless digressions or amplifications "† in the work
of a great poet.

History occupies, in relation to emotion and sentiment,
an intermediate position between literature and science.
It is difficult to watch a game of bowls or a set of tennis
for five minutes without taking sides. How much more
difficult to study great men or great political and social
movements without our sympathies being involved for
or against ! How far is this a sin against history as a
science ? How far, if it is excluded, can we have history
at all ? Here is one view :‡

> The historian, like the judge, should begin with as
> little bias as is humanly possible : . . . But his
> continual effort is towards a definite choice between
> one party or the other ; and if, at the end, he can give
> no guidance to the jury, there must be a certain sense
> of frustration and disappointment.

Such history comes close to advocacy. Perhaps in a
matter in which feeling and interest are so deeply involved—can we view Bannockburn and Flodden except
as Englishmen or Scotsmen,¶ the Reformation except

---

* Pope—*The Dunciad*, ed. J. Sutherland, 1943, p. 363.
† Wickham—*ibid.*
‡ G. G. Coulton—*Four Score Years, An Autobiography*, 1943, p. 323.
¶ Scottish readers may need to be told that most Englishmen, brought up on
Sir Walter Scott, feel about Bannockburn and Flodden as Scotsmen. Both seem
to feel about Waterloo as Frenchmen, for they use that battle—" That was his
Waterloo ! "—as a symbol for final disaster. Such are the paradoxes of feeling.

as Protestants or Catholics, the industrial revolution except as proletarians or bourgeois ?—truth is best reached, as in the law courts, by judgment between competing advocates.

In this connection it is important to realise that our attachment to one side or the other in the controversies of scholarship, science, politics or religion, may have resulted in the first place from some accident of experience. Had we happened to read a different book, attend a different meeting or come in contact with a different teacher, we might have been just as hot on the other side. Some day we do read a different book or in some other way come in contact with a different theory or system of beliefs or values. We may shut our minds to new truth or embrace it with reluctance.

You have learnt something. That always feels at first as if you had lost something.*

The sense of loss comes from the breaking of emotional ties which have been formed for what is now seen to be faulty. In such cases we have lost the lesser and gained the greater. Parties and party allegiances, party controversies and party hatreds, are unavoidable conditions of the debate by which knowledge is advanced.

Where there is much desire to learn, there of necessity will be much arguing, much writing, many opinions ; for opinion in good men is but knowledge in the making.†

Loyalty to a party or a side is not an end in itself. There may even be a gain in having held a contrary opinion.

To become properly acquainted with a truth, we must first have disbelieved it, and disputed against it.‡

---

* G. B. Shaw—*Major Barbara*, Act III.
† J. Milton—*Areopagitica*.
‡ Novalis, q. in Carlyle—*Heroes and Hero-Worship*.

CHAPTER IX

CONCENTRATION AND WILL

Depend upon it, Sir, when a man knows he is to be
hanged in a fortnight, it concentrates his mind
wonderfully.

If the reader will look at what is in front of him, he
will find that he can concentrate his attention upon any
part of his field of vision. Thus he can give his attention,
let us say, to the clock on the mantelpiece, to the position
of the hands, to the figures on the dial, to one of them,
to the clock case, to its design, to the kind of wood it is
made of, to the candle-sticks on either side of it, to the
picture above it, and so on. The effect of such attention
is to give the object greater prominence in the mind,
just as in the theatre the spot-light gives greater prominence to that upon which it is directed.

As the reader turns his attention now to this and now
to that, he will find that his body plays a part. The
eyes move of themselves so that the object attended to is
imaged on the *fovea*, the most sensitive part of the retina
and the centre of clearest vision. His head, or his head
and the rest of his body, may also turn in the new direction. Attention to a sound or a smell is accompanied
by movements correspondingly favourable to the reception of the stimulus attended to, and the same will be
found to hold in the case of the other senses. The aim of
all these movements is to adjust the sense organs to the
stimuli which are being attended to.

Just as some movements are made which are favourable to attention, so others are inhibited which would be

---

Note.—The quotation at the head of the chapter is from: *Boswell's Life of
Johnson*, ed. G. Birkbeck Hill, 1887, Vol. III, p. 167.

unfavourable. In order to hear better we hold our breath.
When we look intently at something, there is a tightening
of the muscles and an increased rigidity of the body,
so that small involuntary movements may not interfere
with our observation of it.   As Mr. George Robey sings,

I *stopped*, and I looked, and I listened.

These adjustments of the body accompany attention,
but they are not the attention itself.   Attention is a
mental and not a bodily act.   The bodily movements
which accompany it are impulsive.   That is to say, we
find ourselves making them without having resolved to
do so. The body, like a good servant, manipulates our
sense organs so as to serve us. The movements are the
consequences of our attention, not the attention itself.

This is easily seen in the case of attention given to a
purely mental object. We may close our eyes and plan
a machine or the furnishing of a room. We may mentally
add up or multiply figures, or consider some theoretical
question upon which sensory experience has little bearing. In such cases there is no part for the sense organs
to play, but there may be muscular tensions which give
to the body a pose characteristic of intense concentration.

In what does this mental act of attention consist ?
First of all in the mental counterparts of the two bodily
responses which accompany it : the image or thought
that is attended to is brought more clearly before us,
and, at the same time, competing or interfering images
or thoughts are pushed aside. To study something we
must " concentrate upon it," " give our attention to it."
Sometimes we try without achieving success. How can
we learn to concentrate at will more effectively ?

At first sight it might seem that some persons have
greater powers of concentration than others, just as
some have stronger muscles, and that they can direct

these powers upon any subject, whether mathematics or grammar, poetry or science, just as a strong man can use his muscles equally well to lift any kind of material, stone or metal, bags of coal or bags of corn. This is not quite so. The boy who sits at the cinema or over an adventure story, so engrossed that he is deaf and blind to everything else, achieves there a degree of concentration which perhaps fails him at lesson time. Thus the problem of improving his concentration upon Latin accidence or the binomial theorem is not that of increasing his general powers of concentration. His need is to develop such powers in relation to his studies as he already possesses in relation to some of his other interests.

This suggests that we do not have one power of attention which can be switched at will from one subject to another, as the spot-light in the theatre can be switched from one character to another on the stage, but that we develop special powers of attention for each subject that we study. This is not quite true either, for some people seem to be much more given to mind wandering than others, whatever the subject ; and the successful prosecution of one line of study may mean an increased power of attacking another subject—if this other subject is not too different in its nature.

The word " concentrate " itself suggests the answer to this problem. It has a military as well as a psychological sense : to concentrate an army is to bring together the different units of which it is composed at the point where their force is to be exerted in attack or defence. A concentration may fail because the commander does not give the right orders or cannot get them obeyed ; it may also fail because the requisite forces are not available. In the same way an attempt to concentrate the attention on some problem may fail because we cannot keep the problem before the mind and summon up the relevant knowledge which we possess ; or it may fail because we do not possess the items of knowledge which are necessary for understanding and solving it.

We can all concentrate upon an interesting story. We expect something good, and we willingly make the little effort of attention that is necessary to embark upon the first sentences—the commander, our will, gives the necessary orders and they are obeyed. We possess the necessary powers of understanding and feeling—the scene opens before our eyes, we hear the spoken words, are anxious or elated, pitiful or angry, according to the events that take place before us. We have concentrated our mental forces effectively to re-create from the printed words the world of the author's imagination.

It may be otherwise with some more specialised piece of writing. Again the will does its work and we make the little effort of attention. But this time we may not possess the necessary powers of understanding, and so we cannot concentrate them. The author uses words which are strange to us and conceptions or principles with which we are insufficiently acquainted. We cannot from his printed words re-create anything at all. Increased effort of attention does not help. Defeat cannot be averted by issuing more and more urgent commands to an army that does not exist. We must postpone the assault until we have recruited the army. That is to say, we must look elsewhere for help and return armed with the vocabulary and the conceptions or principles necessary for understanding this piece of writing. The author assumed the presence of these in his reader's mind, and it is useless to tackle him without this equipment.

The student may not do this. He may persist in his direct attack. What happens ? The greater his effort to understand the words before him, the less they seem to mean. He finds that his mind, instead of being alert and interested, is rapidly becoming a blank. He pulls himself together and tries again—with the same result. He then becomes angry or despondent : that is to say, he begins to respond emotionally. He pushes the book from him with annoyance, as a piece of dull and stupid pedantry, or he blames himself instead of the author, saying, " I am no good at this," or " I suppose I have not the necessary brains." It is clear that progress is impossible along these lines. Where was the initial mistake ? It was in supposing that an intellectual difficulty could be overcome by a greater effort of will, when what was required was not a tremendous effort, but a moderate and reasonable degree of effort exerted in a more effective way. When a motor car engine ceases to function, because a minute piece of dirt has lodged between the platinum points of the make-and-break, the engine cannot be started by great muscular effort at the starting-handle. On the other hand, it can be put right by a very small muscular effort directed to the removal of the little piece of dirt. Something of the same kind is true here.

Why does the student seem to understand the passage less the greater the effort he makes ? This question can be illustrated by an experiment. Let the reader concentrate his attention to the exclusion of everything else upon the word EQUIP which is printed on p. 129. He is to look at it intently, continuously, and with a determination to think of nothing else, not even of topics which the word itself may suggest to him.

He will probably find that at the first glance the word is familiar and unremarkable. As he continues to look at it, it may appear less familiar, till perhaps he begins to doubt whether it is correctly spelt, or even whether

EQUIP

it is an English word at all. If his powers of attention—his ability to concentrate upon these five letters to the exclusion of everything else—are strong, and enable him to carry out the instructions for the experiment, his mind will become a blank even to the letters themselves. He will fall asleep. He will have hypnotised himself.

To perceive or to understand something is to bring to bear upon it our relevant knowledge. To perceive as letters the design of black patches in Fig. 7 is to perceive these in terms of our previous experience of letters. To understand an English sentence is to bring to bear upon it our previous experience of the words that compose it, an experience of them in scores or hundreds or thousands of different connections. The fiat of the will can direct the attention upon a particular object or sentence in order that our relevant experience can be brought to bear upon it. It can also prohibit irrelevant experience from coming into our minds ; but, if there is no relevant experience, no effort of will can create it. If then we force ourselves to attend, the effort of will itself excludes all experience that is irrelevant, there is no relevant experience, and the mind becomes a blank—we go to sleep. Hypnosis—the artificial sleep induced by the hypnotist—may be brought about in much this way. If the reader suffers from insomnia, he may find it useful to practise it upon himself, by relaxing his muscles in an arm-chair or in bed, and concentrating his attention upon some detail in his field of vision. The snag is that, if he suffers from insomnia, he is probably in a condition of fatigue that makes it difficult for him to concentrate his attention to the required degree.

Let us take as an example a sentence which may be unintelligible to a great many readers :

If the mean of a series is greater than the median, there is positive skew, and *vice versa*.

If the reader knows nothing about statistics, he may feel that this sentence means nothing in his life, and the oftener he reads it over and the greater the effort of attention he makes, the less it may seem to mean. If he is familiar with statistics, its meaning will be about as obvious to him as a statement that three fours are equivalent to four threes. If a class of students comes to it with adequate preparation—that is, if they know that " series " means a set of measures of varying magnitude arranged in order, that the " mean " is their arithmetical average, that the " median " is the middle number, when they are arranged in order of magnitude, and that a *frequency* curve is " positively skewed " when, instead of being symmetrical, it is drawn out in the direction of the higher values—the principle expressed in this sentence can be made clear to them in about three minutes, no great effort is required to understand it, and its novelty excites a reasonable degree of interest. This happy result can be reached only by becoming acquainted with the conceptions upon which the understanding of the sentence depends, and by using them until they become working parts of the mind's structure. Then, like good soldiers, they jump to their duty at the word of command.

When such a ready response fails, the fault is not with the mind but with our misuse of it. The mind is ever ready to illuminate as it can whatever is presented to it. This readiness may be shown by another experiment in voluntary attention. In this case the reader is invited to give to the word SHEATHE, printed on p. 133 the same kind of attention which he gave to EQUIP.

He will find as before that consciousness is narrowed until there is an approach to hypnosis. But this word is in one respect different from the other—it readily breaks up into significant parts: SHEathe, sHEathe,

sheAThe, shEAThe, sHEATHe, sheaTHE, sheatHE, SHEATHe, sHEAThe. The mind will ring the changes on these, just as it does on the possible groupings in Fig. 8.

The dependence of these processes upon what is familiar may also be illustrated from this experiment. Thus the everyday words indicated above present themselves most readily. Other combinations—SHEAT, a freshwater fish, and SHEA of the surname, *O'Shea*—are less likely to obtrude themselves, though, if the reader will repeat the experiment, they are more likely to appear, now that his attention has been drawn to them.

In this spontaneous fertility of the mind lie our powers of independent thinking and also our powers of understanding what someone else has thought before us. The function of the will is to direct it to purposes that will be of use, and under conditions that are favourable to success, but it can work only with the tools that previous experience has provided. On the other hand, it lies within our wills to direct attention to the suggestions that come to us in this way, to note them for consideration, to examine and test them, or, if they are slow to come, to turn the problem over in the mind in such a way as to encourage their appearance.

There is another kind of concentration. Walter Leaf, the great banker and Homeric scholar, was once found by a friend, book in hand, in a roomful of romping children. Asked how he could work in such a noise, Leaf replied, " I am not working. I am only learning Persian grammar." The power of disregarding powerful stimuli in order to concentrate the attention on the task in hand, is certainly a useful one, for quiet and seclusion are not always available.

External distractions are not more serious hindrances than competing thoughts and impulses. These may be

SHEATHE

mere temptations to mind wandering as a relief from the pressure of the task in hand. As such they must be resisted, and nothing will be accomplished by one who cannot resist them. On the other hand it does not pay to drive oneself too hard. Perseverance at the same task means an increasing tension, and by and by so much energy may be going into the work of keeping competing thoughts from intruding, that there is a kind of deadlock. It may therefore be better to concentrate on performing a certain unit of work, and then relax before buckling to again. The relaxation may be no more than looking out of the window or walking up and down the room for a few moments, while one's thoughts wander. An eminent scholar, known to the writer, had the habit of writing one paragraph of the work upon which he was engaged and then playing a game of patience, before writing the next paragraph. During the game the next paragraph took shape in his mind. One of the greatest of living novelists used, I am told, to leave his work about once an hour for a short spell on the tennis court. The student will find that it is often during such a period of relaxation that a light will break upon him, that he will suddenly find that he knows what to write next, or what his author means by some hitherto obscure remark, or the bearing upon what he is reading of something he has read elsewhere.

Sometimes a small change in the direction of the attention may have a similar effect. Thus in thinking, as we turn a question over in our minds, different aspects of it come prominently before the attention, and one of these may suggest the solution for which we are seeking. If the reader will turn again to Fig. 3 and observe its changes, he may find that he is able to delay these changes, though he cannot prevent them from taking place. He may also find that he is able to accelerate them by directing his attention now to one part of the figure and now to another. He quite literally " turns the figure over in his mind." By directing attention voluntarily now to one aspect of our topic and now to another we get quite a fresh light upon it.

This experiment brings to our notice the connection between attention and the will. Our attention is only partly under our control. There are certain kinds of stimuli that force themselves upon our attention. A loud noise, because of its loudness, a toothache because of its painfulness, a word of praise, an insult or the threat of danger because they rouse our emotions—such stimuli secure our attention whatever we may be engaged upon. Such attention is called *involuntary* or *enforced*, because it is an attention which we give without, or even against, our will.

Attention which results from a direct act of the will is called *voluntary* attention. The reader had an experience of this in the experiment with the word EQUIP. When we perform an act of voluntary attention either of two things may happen. As in that experiment there may be a narrowing of consciousness ; the object attended to stimulates little or no response from the mind, and the will forbids any straying of the attention to more fruitful objects ; the effort needed to hold the attention to the object becomes greater until the attempt breaks down, either in sleep or in wandering thoughts. It may be consoling to the preacher to reflect that, among those who fall asleep during his sermons, are some who have made the most conscientious endeavours to follow, while, of course, it is also true that some of those who have stayed awake, have been able to do so because they allowed their thoughts to wander.

Our powers of voluntary attention would be of little use to us if they led only to self-hypnotism. An act of voluntary attention, short-lived in itself, is of value because it can set going a more profitable kind of attention. If the object attended to is not a barren one, like the single word, or over our heads, like the sermon, voluntary attention passes into *interested attention*, the attention of the boy at the cinema during a thriller, the attention with which we read a novel, or carry on any activity in which we are interested. It is easy to recognise this kind of attention : it requires no effort and there is no tendency for the thoughts to stray. In the words of Samuel Butler :

> To know whether you are enjoying a piece of music or not you must see whether you find yourself looking at the advertisements of Pear's soap at the end of the programme.*

In study voluntary attention and interested attention are both essential. Without our powers of voluntary attention we should be unable to direct our minds to the subjects which we wish to study. To sit down to work, to pick up a text-book and begin to read, to make a note, to consult a book of reference, to begin by going quickly over yesterday's work, to compare one author's statement with that of another, to adhere to a programme of work or practice, to set about working a series of exercises, to stop and face a difficulty that might be passed over, to persevere with a piece of necessary memorizing when it has become burdensome—all these are explicitly voluntary acts ; in each case, by an act of will, we put the mind and the body into the appropriate attitude for the activity which we intend.† Everything is now ready

---

*S. Butler—*Note-books*, 1918, p. 209.
  † We can greatly facilitate them by having the necessary tools at hand. Reference books and the means of making notes should be within reach of one's chair, so far as this may be possible. Notes should be filed on some system that will allow of their being easily found when wanted. The programme of work should be a reasonable one.

for the appropriate interest to take over. Interest is the driving power, the engine ; voluntary attention is only the steering-wheel.

Where does the interest come from ? From diverse sources. From our primitive instincts,* our natural curiosity, our desire to excel, to receive praise, to surpass others, to feel that we have done ourselves justice, our obstinacy in face of a difficulty, our fear of the consequences of failure, our hatred of being beaten. These primitive tendencies with which we are born, are stimulated by the various objects and situations which we meet with in the course of our lives. We become afraid of this, fond of that, and so on, building these primitive tendencies into more complex structures, called *sentiments*, our loves and hates, likes and dislikes, and, most important from the present point of view, our *interests*. As young children we felt and expressed curiosity as to every aspect of the world around us—addressing to our elders a stream of questions which they answered as best they could, until perhaps they gave up in despair. These questions, if followed up—for every answer leads inevitably in a bright mind to another question—would have led into the territory of every branch of philosophy, science or scholarship, for philosophy, science and scholarship as they exist, are only humanity's incomplete answers to the young child's questions. Whenever such primitive curiosity, directed to some aspect of the world, received partially satisfactory answers, an *interest* was born, an interest in history, in the world and its peoples, in the sun and stars, in birds and beasts, in plants, in our own bodies, in poetry or music. An interest is an impulse to gain further knowledge or skill. It grows with what it feeds on. The more we know about a

*For an account of the instincts in relation to education see James Drever's *Instinct in Man*, 1917, p. 149 ff.

subject, in any real and valuable sense of knowing, the more we want to know about it.

The interest which affords the motive power in study is thus a growing thing with many roots. These are the forces which the will, like a general in the field, concentrates upon the object of attention. That focus of attention is the growing point of the moment. Just as new skill grows out of old skill, so new knowledge grows out of the knowledge we already possess. The new and the old meet in the act of attention. Our control over the process lies in our power to switch our attention now to this and now to that, in order to initiate the processes of interested attention in which mental growth can take place. Thus concentration, in the sense of absorption in the subject one is studying to the point of blindness and deafness to all else, is not the result of strength of will but of strength of interest, the strength of some desire for a particular piece of knowledge, for insight into some complex problem, for the solution of a puzzle or the mastery of a technique.

CHAPTER X

THE TABLE OF THE MEMORY

I've a grand memory for forgetting, David.

Selection is the very keel upon which our mental ship
is built . . . If we remembered everything we should
on most occasions be as ill off as if we remembered
nothing.

I am haunted by single lines, plucked here and there by
infallible instinct; there is no critic like the memory.

Forgetting is a function of the mind as necessary to
us as remembering. If we did not forget, we could not
in any effective sense remember. It is not this useful
elimination of unwanted recollections that attracts our
notice, but the occasions when we cannot recall something that we want to remember, and so forgetting gets
a bad name.

It is probable that everything that happens to us
leaves some permanent impress upon our bodies and
minds. That does not mean that we are able to recall it.
As a result of striking the typewriter keys some tens of
thousands of times, we are able to strike them correctly
with a minimum of effort. Each of these tens of
thousands of occasions has contributed to that result,
but we cannot recall each separate occasion. The
ability to typewrite is useful: the recall of each act that
led to it would not be. Each occasion on which we have
added 5 and 7 and got 12 as the answer, has similarly
increased our speed and accuracy in adding these
numbers, but we cannot recall each of these occasions.

Note.—The quotations at the head of the chapter are from: R. L. Stevenson—
Kidnapped, Ch. XVIII; Wm. James—*Principles of Psychology*, I, 680; J. B.
Yeats—*Passages from the Letters*, ed. E. Pound, 1917.

There is a record* of a young woman of four or five and twenty who in the delirium of a high fever was found to be speaking Latin, Greek and Hebrew in very pompous tones and with most distinct enunciation. She was an innocent and simple creature, unable to read or write. Trick or conspiracy and scholarly knowledge being equally excluded, demoniac possession was put forward as the explanation. A young physician determined to trace her past life step by step, and eventually discovered that the girl had been adopted at the age of nine by an old clergyman, and had lived in his house for some years. It was the old man's custom to walk up and down a passage of his house into which the kitchen door opened, and to read to himself with a loud voice out of his favourite books. The physician succeeded in identifying in these books (which remained in the family) so many of the passages taken down at the young woman's bedside that no doubt could remain as to the origin of her delirious ramblings. We may be able, in a normal state of mind, to recall but little of a lecture, a poem or a play that we have listened to intently. We do not expect to recall anything at all in a language unknown to us. It would seem that in an abnormal mental state more can be recalled than at other times, and therefore that more is recorded in the memory than there is evidence for in normal recall.

There is evidence for this of a less dubious kind. An American psychologist† read twenty lines of the Greek poet Sophocles every day for fifteen months in his child's hearing, beginning when the child was fifteen months old. He then read another passage daily during the next fifteen months, and so on till he had read seven

*S. T. Coleridge—*Biographia Literaria*, Everyman's Library, pp. 59-60.
†H. E. Burtt—*Journal of Genetic Psychology*, 1932.

passages in this manner. The child then learned all these passages by heart, together with three fresh passages. If the reading aloud had had no effect, the new and the old passages should have required an equal amount of effort to get by heart. This was not the case. The passages used for the daily reading needed on the average 317 repetitions each. The new passages needed 435 repetitions. There was therefore a saving of 118 repetitions, or 27 per cent. We must therefore conclude that even such an experience as overhearing a strange and unintelligible language leaves some traces on the mind or nervous system.

Under the artificial conditions of hypnotism or psycho-analysis many memories can be recovered which cannot be recalled in the normal way. They must have been mislaid or inaccessible rather than lost, and presumably each of us has a large mass of such potential memories in his mental lumber-room—material which there has never been any reason for calling to mind, as well as material of a more sinister kind, material akin not to the old junk of the lumber-room but to the skeleton in the cupboard.

How much of our experience do we want to remember ? Every breakfast that we have eaten in forty years ? Every spoonful of porridge and every mouthful of bacon and egg ? Every movement of mastication and swallowing that went with every mouthful ? And so for all our activities ? On such a basis every event of our lives would take exactly as long to remember as it took to live through, and the present would be overwhelmed by the past.

We do not remember every meal that we have eaten, or even every specially interesting meal. Let the reader try to go back year by year and recall all his Christmas dinners. He will certainly remember some. There will certainly be blanks. It is like the representation of a great crowd in a picture : there is an impression of innumerable heads, but on examination it is found that only a limited number—a few prominent ones—are really shown.

What we are able to recall is thus the result of selection. Only the salient features of an event or a period of time are preserved. If the reader will recall his last meal he will find that this process has already begun : he will recall the separate courses, but scarcely the separate mouthfuls, some of the topics of conversation, and perhaps one or two remarks, but not every word that was said.

What he does remember may be a better record of what passed than if his mind preserved every detail, just as we should get a better account of the last war by reading a one volume history of it than by going through the files of a newspaper for the same period, though the latter may be many times as bulky. The historian's account will select. It will emphasise what is important and bring out the significance and inter-relations of events as no contemporary day to day account can do. To compose such a history is an arduous and highly skilled task of selection, compression, arrangement and interpretation. Yet this is just what our memories do for us without our troubling ourselves in the matter. You read a novel and, as you reach the last page, you commend it to a friend. He asks what it is about, and you reply at once with a short summary of the story. The sifting and summarising seems to have been done without the need to take thought.

That is what happens in a well organised mind. There are people in whom this process of selection does not work so efficiently. The events that happen to them make upon their minds a series of impressions in the order in which they happen, each linked to each by linear association. The significant ones cannot be recalled without passing along the chain and recalling the non-significant ones which came in between, and any one of these may involve a further digression along some other irrelevant line of association. A good example of this is to be found in Miss Bates, one of the characters in Jane Austin's *Emma*. The following is an example of her conversation.*

" But where could *you* hear it ? " cried Miss Bates. " Where could you possibly hear it, Mr. Knightley ? For it is not five minutes since I received Mrs. Cole's note—no, it cannot be more than five—or at least ten —for I had got my bonnet and spencer on, just ready to come out—I was only gone down to speak to Patty again about the pork—Jane was standing in the passage—were not you, Jane ?—for my mother was so afraid that we had not any salting-pan large enough. So I said I would go down and see, and Jane said, ' Shall I go down instead ? for I think you have a little cold, and Patty has been washing the kitchen.' ' Oh, my dear,' said I—well, and just then came the note. A Miss Hawkins—that's all I know—a Miss Hawkins of Bath."

The passage is quoted by William James† as an example of

Those insufferably garrulous old women, those dry and fanciless beings who spare you no detail, however petty, of the facts they are recounting, and upon the thread of whose narrative all the irrelevant items cluster as pertinaciously as the essential ones, the slaves of literal fact, the stumblers over the smallest abrupt step in thought. . . .

* Chapter XXI.
† *Op. cit.*—I, 570-1.

Anyone who reads examination scripts will see the same tendency at work in many of them. An examination question has started the student off on some part of his lecture notes that is related to it, and he proceeds to reproduce the topics of the lecture in the order in which they were presented to him, instead of picking out and arranging in his answer the parts which are relevant to the question with which he is dealing. Why does he do this ? It is not because he has forgotten the relevant material, for it sometimes happens that he reproduces some of it in answer to another question—one to which it is irrelevant. It is because in the circumstances of the examination room his memory does not select what is relevant. How may such an unfortunate failure be avoided ? The answer is two-fold. It is concerned with the student's methods of study and with the circumstances of the reproduction.

To take the latter first—the conditions of the examination room demand our sympathy ; time is limited ; much is at stake ; the examinee is probably suffering from some degree of fatigue from over-study : it is not surprising if his mental condition temporarily approximates to that of Miss Bates.

As to preparation, it is mainly a matter of interest. If the student is interested in the subject matter, many different links between this part and that will be evident to him, as he listens to a lecture or reads a book upon the subject. Also, because he is interested, the subject will frequently be in his thoughts—while he is sitting on a bus, taking letters to the post, dressing or, like Archimedes, in his bath. As he turns it over in his mind, he will pass from one instance or principle to another, until the whole is organised in his mind in a systematic way. It is then easy to pass from one point, which is relevant to the question in hand, to another which is equally relevant. In fact the relevant material will come to his mind with little or no effort on his part. If on the other hand he has merely read through his lecture notes conscientiously, but without interest in them, he has merely formed a chain of associations following the order of topics adopted by the lecturer and, when he finds himself in the examination room, there is no time to work along this chain consciously selecting the matter which is relevant.

There is a second kind of forgetting which is less beneficent. Just as a photograph fades or letters cut on a stone are effaced by the weather, so mental impressions, even useful ones, are weakened with the passage of time. It has been found by experiment that the rate of forgetting is most rapid at first. The rate depends upon the nature of the material, the method of learning employed, and other factors. The loss is most rapid for rote memory—that is, for material learned parrotwise, without intelligent understanding. Some material can of course be learned in no other way, because it is not meaningful. To treat meaningful material like this is clearly uneconomical and, if material for learning involves any meaning, this should be stressed in studying it. Where material is meaningful, and its parts are logically interdependent, the loss may then be slight over a long period of time.

These rules are subject to some strange exceptions. What is striking may be impressed upon the memory once and for all. It is a case of " once seen—or heard—never forgotten." This may be due to the strength of the original impression ; or it may be because what is striking is recalled and dwelt upon, or described to someone else, and on each such occasion the original impression is renewed. What strikes one person does not strike another. It is a question of interest, and interest is a matter of the intelligence and previous knowledge that we bring to bear upon what is presented to us. Thus the answer to some question that we have been considering for some time is not likely to be forgotten, when we have at last found it in a book or a lecture, or—best of all for purposes of retention—by thinking it out for ourselves.

A second exception to the rule is the well-known fact that our early memories persist longest. An old man may recall vividly the circumstances of his youth, when the events of his middle life are already dimmed, or when he has difficulty in recalling those of yesterday. It is as if the early memories maintain a degree of vigour which later memories have never possessed.

This suggestion that memories live with a vigour of their own is supported by facts of another kind indicated by William James's remark* that we learn to swim in winter and to skate in summer, that is, during the periods when we are not practising these activities. Most of us have at some time found an improvement in our golf or tennis after a fortnight or so when we have been prevented from going onto the links or the courts. This is not a matter of recovery from fatigue, because the interval may have been a period of vigorous exercise of another kind. It seems as if the nervous apparatus involved has actually become more efficient during this interval.

Memory and active thought are more closely related than is sometimes supposed. Thinking involves remembering ; for to think is to apply our past experience to our present problem. Thus in the case of the hunter who was found shot (p. 98), the solution of the problem depends upon remembering the properties of a burning glass when considering how the gun may have been

---

* *Principles of Psychology*, I, 110.

discharged. On the other hand remembering is far from being a process of mechanical reproduction. We have already seen that memory is selective : when it is working well it sorts out what is relevant. It may do more. It may actually re-shape the material recalled so as to make it more suitable. A small example of this happened to the writer in the composition of Chapter XIII of this book. A quotation occurred to him which he could use to emphasise his point. Reference to the book showed that the two lines were remembered, not as they were written, but in a form more suitable for his purpose (*see* p. 203).

The practical question in the case of memory is how to make the best use of it. To answer this question we must first ask what we want to use it for. It then becomes plain that we do not always want to use it in the same way. It is only very occasionally that we need to recall something in the sense of getting it back from our memories as we should get it by referring to a book. It is therefore only very occasionally that we need learn anything " by heart." The mind cannot compete with a reference book, either in accuracy or comprehensiveness, and should not be used as a substitute for one.

> . . . a man should keep his little brain attic stocked with all the furniture that he is likely to use, and the rest he can put away in the lumber room of his library, where he can get it if he wants it.*

A simple example of memorising is to be found in the multiplication table. This sets out in orderly fashion seventy-two arithmetical operations (two times one, two times three, etc., up to nine times nine) and the resulting products. Each of these products can be discovered by simply counting—count out six beans or matches or

---

* Conan Doyle—*Op. cit.* 'The Adventure of the Five Orange Pips.'

counters, and then another six and then another six ; then count the lot, and you have the answer to the question : What is three times six ? To do our computation in this way would be tedious, so we proceed to make a little reference book—we write down the seventy-two questions and the answers to them. We can now multiply any number by any other by referring to our reference book, our multiplication table, just as we refer to a table of logarithms, or the tables used for calculating wages or income tax.

Anyone who did this systematically would find that reference to the table would soon become unnecessary for some of the items, because the number he wanted came into his mind before he looked for it. Since the total number of items is not very large—seventy-two, if we count two fours and four two's as separate items, thirty-six if we count each such pair as one item*—he would soon be independent of the printed table altogether.

The multiplication table contains facts which we use every day, so that it is worth while to have it at our finger ends. It is not worth while to learn the table of logarithms. For four-figure tables this would mean 1,710 items. It is therefore more convenient to refer to the table. Thus the question what to learn is a practical one, involving two considerations : how much there is to learn and how often, or how urgently, the information will be wanted.

How then should such a set of facts be learned ? There is one safe rule : Learn the material as nearly as possible in the way in which you are going to use it. This usually means : Don't learn it by heart, but practise yourself in applying it. In the case of the multiplication

---

* These are all that we *need* for multiplication. The twelve times table is useful in this country, because there are twelve pence in a shilling. The ten times can be reduced to a simple principle—add a nought to the multiplicand. The eleven times has little importance.

table the common practice is to begin by learning to
" repeat " it. This is a waste of time and energy. No
one ever wants to repeat the multiplication table, except
perhaps a teacher teaching someone to repeat it. What
we want is to recall 27 directly in response to 9×3,
21 directly in response to 7×3, 12 directly in response
to 4×3, etc. These items will in practice occur in
random order. In learning to " say " the tables we are
forming a number of unnecessary associations. In the
following three items of the table the associative bonds
represented by the thinner arrows are necessary for
" saying " the tables, but unnecessary for any other
purpose.

$$(1 \times 3) \Rightarrow 3 \rightarrow (2 \times 3) \Rightarrow 6 \rightarrow (3 \times 3) \Rightarrow 9$$

In computing we want to get from (2×3) to 6, and
from (3×3) to 9, but never from 6 to (3×3) nor from
9 to (4×3).*

This in itself is bad enough, but worse follows. Having
memorised the tables, it is still necessary to learn to
apply them. What happens is something like this. We
require, let us say, three times eight. The answer does
not come to mind at once, so the learner begins to repeat
the table from the beginning " three ones are three,
three fours are twelve, three fives are fifteen " until he
comes to the item he wants. Thus, having learned to
recite the table, he has still to learn to respond appropriately to the separate items. He might have been
learning to do this in the time spent in learning to recite
the tables by heart. He would then have been free
from a set of bad habits from which many of us never
free ourselves—getting the item which we want by
reciting to ourselves those which precede it in the table,
and so wasting time and increasing the possibility of error.

* cf. D. Kennedy-Fraser—*The Education of the Backward Child*, p. 215 ff.

These principles are of such great importance and general application that it is worth while to illustrate them from another subject. To learn historical dates, as is so often done, by connecting the name of each event with the year in which it occurred is a dull, laborious and almost useless process. Yet is it necessary to carry a certain number of dates in one's mind in order to study history at all. What, and how much, and for what purpose, are the questions we should ask. In the first place, it is necessary to have a general framework—a framework that spans the centuries of recorded history and merges into the archæological, and finally the geological, record. This general frame of reference must then be amplified by a more detailed framework for the country or period in which we are interested. These frames of reference have no more value than a library catalogue without a library, unless the dates which have been learned have a background of knowledge—know-ledge of events, persons, dress, arms, architecture, literature, social organisation, methods of government— to which they are points of reference. This frame of reference then gives meaning to each fresh date that one meets with, and the more useful of these dates are assimilated into it.

Thus when we read that Alexander Pope was born in 1688 and died in 1744 we know that his childhood was lived under William III, that his youth and early man-hood coincided with the reign of Queen Anne, and that his maturity came in the reigns of George I and George II. To read that the *Epistle to Augustus* was published in 1737 is to infer that it was addressed to George II, that Pope was then 49, that Walpole and the Whigs were in power, that it is the year before the appearance of Johnson's *London*, that it is among the last of his works. Having noted these implications of the date, it may be unnecessary to recall the date itself. To be able to recall it, if it does not carry such implications, has little, if any, value.

The multiplication table has to be recalled in bits and not as a whole. Sometimes we want the whole of something and not the bits—for example a poem. A poem is a unity in which the parts take their meaning largely from their place in the whole, and we want to be able to recall the successive lines and stanzas in their order. Experiment has shown that in such cases it is better to learn the material as a whole—to read the poem through from beginning to end until it is known. Here, curiously, traditional school practice is to learn such material in sections, a stanza or a part of a stanza at a time. The apparent advantage of this method lies in the feeling that progress is being made, but this advantage is dearly purchased. The corresponding disadvantage of learning a poem as a whole is that we may read it through a good many times before we feel that we have retained any of it, and this may be discouraging, especially if we are reading the poem only in order to learn it, and not because we are interested in it to the point of fascination. If we are so interested, we read it and re-read it with delight, fragments of it come back to us when the book is not at hand and we make great efforts to recall a few more words or phrases. We refer to the book at the first opportunity, and we soon have the whole thing by heart, without seeming to have taken any trouble in the matter.

Should we wish to learn a poem deliberately, and do this by reading it through from beginning to end a sufficient number of times, we are likely to find that we know the beginning and the end some time before we know the middle. We can meet this difficulty by then giving special attention to the parts that we know least.

In learning anything by heart, each repetition deepens the impression made upon our minds, and so makes recall easier. But there is more in the matter than mere repetition. It has been shown that someone may read a list of words aloud many times and yet remember very few of them, if he has read them through, not with a view to recalling them, but for some other purpose. Fewer repetitions would have resulted in many more words being remembered, if there had been an endeavour to learn them. This points to what is generally recognised as one of the best methods of learning—as soon as you have some acquaintance with the material, attempt to recite it without looking at the book and get someone to prompt you—or refer to the book—when you fail. The superiority of this method comes from the effort made to recall what is partially learned, and the specially concentrated attention given to it when you are prompted or refer to the book. Interest, effort, attention—these are the important factors.

The schoolboy doing his evening preparation learns his vocabularies or his declensions till he can just say them. Conscience is satisfied, and he turns his attention to something more attractive. Next day in class he finds that he is no longer word perfect. The explanation is that, as soon as a period of learning terminates, a process of forgetting begins, so that, if we learn something until we can just say it, we have fallen below that level by the next day. This kind of forgetting follows definite laws. It has been found by experiments in which the subject learned sets of nonsense syllables—that is, such combinations of two consonants and a vowel as BEM DUT CAV WIR—that after the first half hour only half the material can be recalled, after eight hours only one-third and after a month only one-fifth.* Thus the rate of forgetting is greatest at first and declines rapidly.

This does not mean that these proportions have been totally lost. They have fallen below the level at which they can be recalled, but a relatively small number of further repetitions will renew their efficiency. Had this additional number of repetitions been made while the material could still be recalled, it would not have been lost within this period of time. This suggests the means which the schoolboy can take to be word perfect at the hour at which he is to be tested. When he is first capable of reproducing the material correctly, he must continue with further repetitions. These, since they follow the stage at which the initial learning is complete, are described as *over-learning*.

Verbal material which we learn is subject to rapid loss when we cease to practise it. This is not true of skills. Thus a skater may soon find himself almost as expert as ever on the ice, although he has not had skates on his feet for fifteen or twenty years. The same is true of typing, dancing, piano playing, or skill at a game. The reason is that when we have learned such movements we repeat them over and over again, many tens or hundreds of thousands of times. Thus we over-learn them heavily. We do this either because we enjoy the movement, as in the case of skating or dancing, or because it is useful, as in the case of typing or knitting. If we enjoy a poem we over-learn it heavily by repeating it to ourselves. With other types of material there may be no such enjoyment. We can however adopt various methods of making a game out of the repetitions—a competition with another learner, or an endeavour to improve on our own previous record.

There are some things worth carrying in one's head which are in their nature confusing. Thus there are 4 gills in a pint, 2 pints in a quart, 4 quarts in a gallon and, if we want to recall how many pints there are in a quart, we may be quite sure that it is either 2 or 4 but uncertain which. If we have noticed that the 2 and the 4 alternate, that " quart " is a form of " quarter," that therefore there are 4 quarts in a gallon, we are not likely to have further difficulty. In all such cases it is well to look for some such rational connection. It is then possible to reconstruct the rest of the pattern from the pieces of it which we are able to recall. Establishing an arbitrary connection is less helpful. Indeed it only adds to the number of things to be remembered. Mr. Jones is to remember to call at the fishmonger's on leaving his office. In order that he may not forget, he ties a knot in his handkerchief. He may forget to look at his handkerchief, or he may find himself looking at the knot and wondering what it was to remind him to do. He really needs two more memory prompters to help him with these two difficulties.

Everybody remembers the names of Charles II's ministers of 1667 because the initials of their names make the word *Cabal* and led to their being so nicknamed. Anyone seriously studying such a period of English history must necessarily become acquainted with the names of ministers in the course of his reading. If he is not so engaged, he has little need to memorize the successive ministries which have governed England, and the ministry of 1667 has by an accident obtained a hold upon our minds out of proportion to its importance. When as a schoolboy I first heard the names of the five rivers of the Punjab, I invented a jingle to link them together. I have retained it ever since, but I cannot recall a single occasion on which this information has been of any use to me.

Such *mnemonics*, or arbitrary memory aids, are a last resort for something which must be retained and which we have failed to learn in a more rational way. In making such a device it is best to look for connections as rational or near-rational as can be found. Another device is to use metre and rhyme. Then only the right word—the word we want to recall—will fit into the pattern.

A mnemonic may be used as a temporary device—a crutch to make use of until a process of learning is complete. Thus a ship's officer at sea should respond to another ship's lights with the appropriate helm order without having to stop and think. He may begin by learning Thomas Gray's ingenious rhymes, of which the following are examples :—

> Green to green and red to red,
> Perfect safety, go ahead.

and :

> If to your starboard red appear,
> It is your duty to keep clear.

He may feel more comfortable because he knows he can fall back upon them at need. But he had better make these rules into automatic responses, before he finds himself making port in thick weather. The same is true of mnemonics in linguistics. The sound of *ee* in *need* is sometimes represented in English spelling by *ie* and sometimes by *ei*. The latter form is the invariable one after c, the former in all other cases except *weir*, *weird*, *inveigle*, *seize* and a number of proper names. The well-known rhyme that states these two rules is useful, but it does not help us with the exceptions, that is, with the words most likely to cause difficulty. Also writing would be a slow process, if we had to recall our spelling in this way. We could not speak a language, or even write it, with any fluency, if dependent on such devices for its grammatical usages. It is a question whether it is not better to learn the appropriate response directly without wasting time in an initial dependence on the crutch.

Repetitions do not make their impressions upon the mind in a mechanical way, like dripping water wearing away a stone. Interest, boredom, fatigue, and processes which go on without our being aware of them, all play their part. The consequence is that the same number of repetitions may give very different results according to the way in which the repetitions are arranged. The most profitable time for learning is when mind and body are vigorous. Since routine work is less affected by fatigue it should be left to the less favourable periods of the day or week. Thus if study must be combined with earning a living the student will gain by studying early in the morning rather than late at night—less time and effort will accomplish as much. It may also secure quiet for a student who has not a room of his own to work in. It is nevertheless a somewhat chilly suggestion.

There is an exactly contrary principle. The retention of what has been learned in one working period is unfavourably affected by the study of similar subject matter in the next working period, less unfavourably by subject matter of a different kind, less unfavourably again by recreative activities, and least unfavourably by sleep. Thus there is some advantage in looking over work just before bed-time, if it does not interfere with sleep.

If the material is of such a kind that interest passes quickly into boredom, it is better to keep the periods of work short—and have a larger number of them. An effective attention is then maintained more easily and both time and effort are saved. Fig. 15 shows the results of an experiment* in which four groups of subjects worked at the same task, substituting numbers for letters, and for the same length of time, a total of two

* Starch, D., *Periods of Work in Learning*, J. Ed. Psy., iii, 4.

hours.   Their speed of work increased throughout, as they learned to associate each letter with the appropriate number.   The graph shows the rate of increase for each group.   The first group who worked in spells of ten minutes twice daily progressed most rapidly.   The second group, working daily spells of twenty minutes progressed less rapidly, but ultimately overtook them.   The third group, working three spells of forty minutes, and the

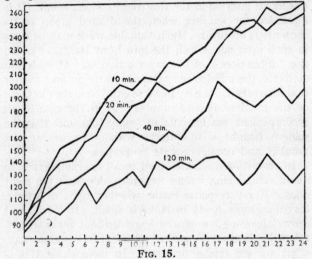

FIG. 15.

fourth group, working for one hundred and twenty minutes without a break, are clearly not getting the same advantage from the time and effort given to the task.* For work of a different kind a different length of period would be desirable.   Ten minute spells would obviously be too short for reading a scientific or philosophical subject.   They may be long enough for any kind of memorising.

* Starch, D., *Pierods of Wаok in Learning*, J. Ed. Psy., iii, 4.

A useful device for securing frequent short repetitions is to write the material on cards or slips of paper which can be carried in the waistcoat pocket. In this way a grammatical rule, a group of words in a foreign language, a mathematical formula, the main dates of a campaign or of a biography, a group of geographical facts, or the like may be readily memorised. A card is taken out unobtrusively on a bus, while waiting in a shop, or during an interval in the theatre or concert room. It is discarded for another when the desired grasp of its contents is attained. Much valuable work may be done in such intervals, which the late Lord Haldane* called the " interstices " of his day's activities. At such odd moments the mind turns naturally to the subject matter that interests it. It may be verse enjoyed in recollection ; or the manipulation of numbers, as in the case of an accomplished mathematician, who told me that he seldom bought a bus ticket without examining its number and considering its properties.

In repetition and attempted recall it is important to avoid establishing wrong responses alongside the right ones. Every response made, whether right or wrong, leaves us more ready to make it again. In " trial and error " learning we cannot learn without making mistakes, because we do not know, except in a general way, what we are trying to learn. In memorising this is otherwise, and we should take every care not to make any errors, or to see that they are corrected at once. Otherwise we have mis-learning and interference.

It is not always evident that mis-learning is taking place. A child is working examples in multiplication by 7. On three occasions he makes the mistake of saying to himself " seven nines are fifty-six," and he is, in consequence of his twenty minutes of practice, a little

---

* Addressing the W.E.A. at Gosport in 1921.

more likely to make this mistake in future. The fact that his answer is marked wrong, and he must do the work over again, does not undo the harm. In fact it may increase it, since he will probably once again hesitate between fifty-six and sixty-three, so that each tendency is a little strengthened, whereas we want one to be made to predominate over the other. The reader has probably had such an experience as this. He is uncertain whether to write *acommodate, accomodate* or *accommodate;* he hesitates between *Don!-at-us* and *Don-at!-us;* he cannot decide whether *The Origin of Species* was published in 1856 or 1859. He looks it up. Next day he finds himself as much in doubt as ever. During the period of hesitation he has dwelt now on one alternative now on the other, thus strengthening each of them without giving either the advantage. The moment spent in looking at the work to which he refers has little influence upon these deeper impressions. If, however, he will note the correct thing on one of his waistcoat pocket cards, and look at it half a dozen times during the next day or two, he will give it the advantage, and it will not trouble him again.

The student should avoid the popular illusion that we have something called a " memory " which can be strengthened by practice, as we strengthen our muscles by exercising them. Experimental results do not bear out this theory. They indicate that to memorize any one kind of material—say, numbers, or nonsense syllables, or verse, or prose, or dates, or place-names, or the words of a foreign language—improves our ability to memorize material *of that kind*. This is not because practice increases our powers of retention. It is probably because we improve our methods of attacking material of that particular kind—for example, we may learn to make use of rhythm, to note resemblances and differences, to use appropriate mnemonic devices. Such improved methods may not be applicable to other kinds of material, and this is probably the reason why practice in learning one kind of material may actually result in a *decrease* in our ability to memorize material of another kind. If then, the student wants to improve his ability to memorize material of a certain kind, he can do this best by memorizing that kind of material, and not by formal memory exercises, which are likely to be either a waste of time or actually harmful.

Only a relatively small amount of material requires to be memorized by these deliberate techniques. Of far greater importance and amount are the residual effects of reading, construing, translating, decyphering, collating, summarising, observing, measuring, dissecting, criticising, calculating, proving, testing, constructing—the active rather than the passive processes of study. The results of these processes are largely below the level of conscious recall. In a perfectly literal sense the most important part of a man's education consists in what is left over after he has forgotten what he learned at school. The reading of a book may have materially altered our outlook and understanding, and it may therefore be affecting our judgments and decisions, after we have forgotten the occasion of reading it, its words, its appearance and its author's name.

In many cases this means that, although the content of some piece of learning has gone, the general pattern remains. The following* is a good as well as an amusing example of a recollection, subject to this degree of decay:

" One of the Georges," said Psmith, " I forget which, once said that a certain number of hours' sleep a day—I cannot recall for the moment how many— made a man something, which for the time being has slipped my memory."

---

* P. G. Wodehouse—*Enter Psmith*, Chapt. XV.

Such memories may be very valuable if at need we can fill in the lost detail by applying to the source from which we have derived them originally. It may be much more important to know one's way about a considerable number of works on a subject, so as to be able to put one's hands, as occasion arises, on what one wants, than to carry a greater amount of one of them in one's mind.

Knowledge is of two kinds. We know a subject ourselves, or we know where we can find information upon it.*

Hilaire Belloc's *Warfare in England* may afford an illustration of memories which function below the level of explicit recall. This little book gives an account of all the important military operations in Britain between the Roman conquest and 1746. There is one factor common to all these campaigns—the geography of the island. Within the period there were changes in the weapons used, but no great change in the speeds of marching armies or their transport. Thus for one campaign after another there are common factors—the importance of London as the lowest crossing of the Thames or as a centre of population, trade and government, the backbone of the Pennines, forest and marsh areas, the three routes into Scotland, the convergence of roads upon Falkirk and Stirling. A study of a general history of England may leave the student's mind in considerable confusion as to the strategy of the various campaigns. Belloc reveals a small number of re-current patterns, into one of which each campaign fits in some respects, and from which it diverges in significant ways. Instead of confusion there is rational order, and a single rapid reading of the book may entirely alter the student's subsequent appreciation of the military history

* *Boswell's Johnson. ed. cit.*—II, 365.

of the island—with grateful memories of Belloc—
and also his approach to the military side of history in
other countries, with perhaps a less conscious indebtedness.

In geography itself the memorising of names—though
we must know some names in order to know any geography at all—may be of much less value than conceptions of general application. To understand what is
meant by a *Mediterranean climate* is to have in one's
hands a tool for thinking about other parts of the world
than the Mediterranean. To memorize the names of
obscure villages in Afghanistan or North Africa may be
a waste of time. To be able to use a gazetteer and read
a map will enable us to master quickly and easily the
geography of any part of the world that unexpectedly
comes into the news or our reading. Such needs cannot
be anticipated by the former method of study.

In other cases it may be desirable to be able to recall
the outline of a book, while retaining only a few striking
examples or arguments under each heading. For this
purpose it is necessary to make out the structure of the
book and, if it is a case of serious reading, to make a
summary. To make a good summary it is necessary to
understand the author's aim and method, to distinguish
the use made of his authorities, his own hypotheses, the
evidence he brings forward, the way he meets criticisms.
It may be well worth while to memorize such a summary
—even to invent a mnemonic for the heads of it. On
the other hand the work of making it has probably
rendered memorizing unnecessary, as it will be impressed
almost as permanently upon the mind as upon the paper.

Part IV
THE TOOLS OF STUDY

CHAPTER XI

WORDS

" When *I* use a word," Humpty Dumpty said in rather a scornful tone, " it means just what I choose it to mean—neither more nor less."

" The question is," said Alice, " whether you *can* make words mean so many different things."

" The question is," said Humpty Dumpty, " which is to be master—that's all."

In his [Sterry's] sentences words are commonly no mere arbitrary symbols for abstract thoughts, but living things that dance and glitter and sing : . . .

          . . . visionary power . . .
Embodied in the mystery of words.

First among the student's tools come words. The greater part of what we learn from others comes to us through the medium of words, and they are largely the vehicle of our own thinking. Because so much of the student's activities consists in the manipulation of words, there is an ever present danger that they may usurp the place of the things they stand for, so that studies may degenerate into verbalism. Such learning is little better than parrot-learning—acquiring words without acquiring the meanings that go with them. It is therefore important to understand how word and meaning are linked, that we may not " darken counsel by words without knowledge."

There are two ways in which words may be used—the

Note.—The quotations at the head of the chapter are from : Lewis Carroll—*Alice Through the Looking-Glass*, Ch. VI ; V. de S. Pinto—*Peter Sterry* 1934, p. 69; Wm. Wordsworth—*The Prelude*, ll 595-7.

scientist's way and the poet's way. These require two different attitudes on the part of a reader. For the scientist, as for Humpty Dumpty, a word is a counter to which he may give exactly the value which is convenient for his purpose. It is a *term*, a tool to reason with, and valid reasoning requires that a term shall not vary its meaning in the course of an argument. Now all words in common use have a long and varied history during which they have served a variety of purposes and so gathered to themselves many meanings or shades of meaning. It is this rich variety of meaning that poetry makes use of, and so the scientific and literary ways of using words are in sharp contrast.

In exact description or in reasoning—that is to say, in the scientific way of writing—our feelings are irrelevant. It is the qualities and characteristics of the thing the word stands for that are important. To refer to these without any possibility of ambiguity a word must have a fixed meaning.

Shoes are made of leather.
Blacksmiths make shoes for horses.
Blacksmiths must therefore work in leather.

The word " shoe " has here two meanings. The first statement is true if we are speaking of the shoes bought in shoe-shops. The second statement is true of shoes of a different kind, horse-shoes. The conclusion is ridiculous. This example is chosen for its obvious absurdity, but a word may vary its meaning in a serious argument without the variation being at all obvious, and so we slip from one meaning to the other without realising it. The terms used in the philosophical and social sciences are particularly liable to such ambiguities, but no science is free from difficulties of this kind.

It is therefore necessary in these studies to tie down

each term to the one sense in which it is to be used in the course of the argument : it must be *defined*. Sometimes this is done in such a way that the reader cannot miss the definition. Thus Euclid begins his book by setting out the terms that he is going to use and his definitions of them, and whenever he brings in a further term, he does so with a little formal ceremony of introduction ; he defines it. Sometimes a writer not only defines a term in the sense in which he is going to use it, but discusses at length the senses in which other writers have used it, and his reasons for preferring his own definition. Such passages are often dull reading for a student beginning a subject. He should note the sense in which the term is to be used in the work itself, and return to the discussion when he has read enough of the subject to be interested in it. Sometimes a writer, fearful of putting the reader off with a formal definition, defines a term incidentally, or by implication, so that it requires a little trouble on the reader's part to find out just in what sense he is using it. Sometimes the reader is left to gather the meaning of a term from the context in which it occurs. In this book the term *stimulus* has been used a number of times, but nowhere defined. The passages in which it occurs may be traced through the index. The reader may refer to these and attempt to frame a definition, which he may then compare with the definition given at the end of this chapter.

A writer may not define a term, because he is using it in a sense which he assumes will be familiar to his reader. In such a case a student may find himself in difficulties. His first resort may be a dictionary. Sometimes, if the term is a technical one, this may not help him very much. He must refer to a text-book of a more general or elementary character, or to a special dictionary devoted to the technical terms of the subject. Occasionally a writer may use a term without having himself made up his mind as to the sense in which he is using it, and this may lead to much discomfiture on the part of the reader, who begins to wonder whether he or the writer is at fault.

Terms which offer no difficulty to one reader may be insuperable obstacles to another. My own knowledge of cricket includes nothing more than what may be learned from occasionally on a fine day watching from a distance for a few minutes :

> . . . the run-stealers flicker to and fro.

Opening Sir Pelham Warner's *The Book of Cricket* at random, I found the following sentence :

> The *pull* differs from the *hook* in that it is more in the nature of a *drive*.

I know what these terms mean on the golf course. But these senses will not do here, for at golf a *drive* may be either a *hook* or a *pull*, as these are terms for ways in which a drive may *go wrong*. The dictionary does not help. The author does not explain these terms, for he was not writing for me, but for someone who might be presumed to know what they mean. His statement will not give me any information until I have found out their meanings from a more elementary book, or from a friend who plays cricket.

A word and its meaning may both be new. *Hormone, autacoid, endocrine, vitamine* are terms invented by scientists to stand for new conceptions at which they had arrived in the course of their work. In other cases an old word may have to carry a new meaning. *Valve, receiver, listener, amplify* and *aerial* have acquired new meanings with the coming of wireless. *Car* has a meaning for us which it did not have before the invention of the internal combustion engine. " He is about to fly to South America " would have had only a few years ago a sinister meaning which it does not have to-day. Such a word as *grace* or *charity* has a long history in several languages during which its meaning has been enriched with the growth of religion, art and philosophy, particularly, in the case of these two words, by the Christian senses which they bear to-day.* The opposite process of impoverishment may also take place. Thus *charity* is now commonly used in the sense of giving alms, instead of in the noble sense of St. Paul,† so that in the Revised Version of the Bible *love* is used in place of it.

In reading a scientific or philosophical work it is necessary to note carefully the sense in which a word is to be used and, whenever the word occurs subsequently in that book, we must read it in that sense, deliberately divesting it of all its other meanings. This may call for a considerable modification of the sense which we have previously attached to it. Such words as *metal, force, acid, complex, instinct, fish, insect* are in common use in senses not precisely defined. Scientifically an insect has six legs and a body divided into head, thorax and abdomen, the latter character being implied by the term itself, which means by derivation *cut-in*. This definition excludes spiders and centipedes, which are quite commonly referred to as insects. *Complex* is a technical term of psychology, now commonly used in the newspapers in a sense, or no-sense, which it would be difficult to define. An *instinct* is an inherited tendency. Everyday speech and writing describe as *instinctive* any act which is done without previous deliberation, whether it is of innate origin or not. A *metal* is for a child a solid, hard, shiny, heavy, cold substance. As he grows older he has to alter his conception of the term—by dropping " heavy " when he meets with aluminium, " solid "

---

* Owen Barfield—*History in English Words*, 1926.
† I Corinthians, xiii.

when he meets with mercury, " hard " when he meets with sodium. Presently, when he studies chemistry, he will find it defined by the characters of opacity, ductility, or malleability and lustre, that it is an element, melts when heated, conducts electricity, and displaces hydrogen in acids.

Because of the different ways in which words are used, a student of science, accustomed to the use of terms in senses previously defined, may be at a loss when he tries to read a piece of literature. In the same way the student of literature who comes to a scientific work may find himself at sea because he is alive to subtle associations, which words bring with them and which the scientific writer ignores. Such a reader gives his attention to these overtones of meaning, and they produce for him a confused jangle instead of a harmony, while at the same time he misses the meaning intended by the writer, or some important part of it.

Literature, even the most moving or the most profound, consists of words, and of words only. This at first appears rather a chilling statement, but a moment's consideration shows its truth. All that the poet has done is to arrange words upon paper ; and that is all that we, his readers, have before us. On the one hand is the poet's experience—that which he has seen or thought, felt or imagined, and this is perhaps the true poem ; on the other is the reader's experience—all that comes to life in our minds as we read. How can such a miracle be performed through the medium of words ?

In the first place we must note that the miracle may be in different degrees an incomplete one, for the poet's experience—the thoughts and feelings for which he has found an expression in his poem—may be very imperfectly re-created in the reader's mind. They can be re-created only out of the reader's experience, and therefore within the limits of his powers of thinking and feeling. However wide these limits may be, his experience of life must differ from that of his author, and out of different materials he cannot build an identical structure. Where each reader forms his own picture, it is impossible to say that any one of these is the writer's. The same is true of understanding and feeling. Thus a poem may have a very different value even for the same reader at different periods of his life. What thrilled him at fifteen may seem cheap and tawdry at twenty-five. What bored him at school, because he then lacked the knowledge or experience of life necessary to appreciate it, may move him profoundly in his maturity. According to Pope :*

A perfect judge will read each work of wit
With the same spirit that its author writ : . . .

The perfect judge is not to be found. Each of us must create, as best he can, out of such mental resources as he possesses, an æsthetic experience which is for him the " meaning " of the poem. How do words enable us to do it ?

" Midnight " in a scientific sense is the point of time when the sun is 180° from our meridian or that of Greenwich. It is important as the zero point from which we reckon the time of day. How little this has to do with the part it plays in any of the following lines !†

Tis the yeares midnight, and it is the dayes, . . .

At the midnight in the silence of the sleep-time, . . .

The iron tongue of midnight hath told twelve ; . .

---

* *Essay on Criticism*, 11, 233-4, Everyman's Library.
† The quotations are from :—J. Donne—*A Nocturnal upon S. Lucies Day*; R. Browning—*Asolando*, 'Epilogue'; W. Shakespeare—*A Midsummer Night's Dream*, V, i; J. Keats—*Ode to a Nightingale*; W. B. Yeats—*The Lake Isle of Innisfree*; W. Shakespeare—*Henry IV*, Part 2, III, ii; *ib.*—*Twelfth Night*, II, iii *ib.*—*Henry IV*, Part 1 1I, iv; J. Milton—*Comus*; *ib.*—*l'Allegro*; W. Shakespeare —*Macbeth*, IV, i.

> To cease upon the midnight with no pain, . . .

> There midnight's all a glimmer, and noon a purple glow, . . .

> We have heard the chimes at midnight.

> . . . not to be a-bed after midnight is to be up betimes ; . . .

> What doth gravity out of his bed at midnight ?

>> Midnight shout, and revelry
>> Tipsy dance, and Jollity.

> Hence loathed Melancholy,
>> Of Cerberus and blackest midnight born, . . .

> How now, you secret, black, and midnight hags !

The word has gathered many associations and many shades of feeling from the many contexts in which it has been met. Some of these are in pronounced contrast, associations of revelry on the one hand and of darkness and horror on the other. Which of them is to give its colour to the word in a particular case depends upon the setting in which we find it. The mental process is the same as that by which the word " hard " brings to mind two different conceptual meanings in two different sentences (p. 64), but in this case it is the accompanying feelings rather than the meaning in the narrower sense of the word that is important.

One of Mr. Aldous Huxley's most brilliant passages* illustrates this most aptly. It concerns the word *carminative*. The young poet, Denis, explains that he has just had a whole poem ruined because this word does not mean what it ought to mean. He had met it first in childhood in connection with tincture of cinnamon and it seemed to him (I paraphrase) to describe the internal glow produced by that fierce and fiery golden liquid. It

---

* *Chrome Yellow*, Chapter XX.

carried vague suggestions of *caro*, of carmine, carnival and carnation, of song, of roses, of sunlight and festival, of the intoxication of love or wine. And he wrote :

And passion carminative as wine. . . .

But then a faint suggestion of doubt sent him in the dictionary, and this magical aura was dispelled by the unromantic medical meaning of the word.

But the dictionary by itself will not do either. The dictionary definition of a *bastard** as " a child born out of wedlock or of adultery" would not make you aware that this word may come quite appropriately in Shakespeare's *King Lear* or Mr. Shaw's *St. Joan*, as the surname of one of your acquaintances or in a legal document, but must not usually be pronounced in general conversation, and may on the other hand be used (under the stress of strong feelings) in ways which will arouse even stronger feelings in those to whom it is applied. Yet all these are important aspects of it. In using words we are guided by an intimate acquaintance with them, gained by meeting them in many different settings, in which different sides of their characters have been revealed to us. We therefore know them as living things. In the dictionary they are as dead as butterflies on pins in a museum. A foreigner who has studied the list of masculine and feminine nouns in his English grammar, and then gone on to learn that he has not been insulted when someone calls him " a lucky dog," is in a position of grave danger next time he wishes to offer congratulations to a lady. It is unwise to refer to the son of a French acquaintance as a *garçon* in his presence, or to tell a French lady in either language that she is a witch. An English lady in Italy, wishing to buy a single ticket, asked at the booking-office for *uno biglietto celibe* (a

---

* Concise Oxford Dictionary.

celibate ticket). A printed appeal to English and American tourists in Italy read :

> Help the Little Sisters of the Poor.
> They harbour all kinds of diseases and have no respect for religion.

One can learn to use a language, the mother tongue or another, only by meeting its words and idioms as living things in real situations. Even then one may slip up. Dr. Johnson unintentionally drew a titter from his hearers* by remarking in commendation of a lady's character :

> . . . the woman had a bottom of good sense.

When he corrected this :

> Where's the merriment ? I say the *woman* was *fundamentally* sensible.

he substituted another word carrying the same double meaning, but with a different emotional connotation.

We may note next the values that words have on account of their sounds. In the days when geography was taught as a dull list of facts to be memorized, the one oasis in that desert was, for the child with an ear for such beauties, in the sound of place-names.

> When I was but thirteen or so
> I went into a golden land,
> Chimborazo, Cotopaxi
> Took me by the hand.†

Place names have a special value in poetry, because the poet is more or less free to choose them for their sound— almost as free as the artist is in choosing colours and shapes for a formal design.

---

* *Boswell's Life*, ed. cit., IV, 99.
† W. J. Turner—" Romance " in *The Hunter, and other Poems*. 1916.

Where the great vision of the guarded Mount
Looks toward Namancos and Bayona's hold ;* . . .

That the geographical meaning of these names may be
doubtful does not detract from their contribution to the
music of the lines.   Dr. Johnson says of Pope :†

I have been told that the couplet by which he
declared his own ear to be most gratified, was this :
        Lo where Mæotis sleeps, and hardly flows
        The freezing Tanais thro' a waste of Snows, . . .
But the reason for this preference I cannot discover.

The reader may judge for himself whether we must
think Pope either incorrectly reported or false in
judgment.

With other words the poet may not be so free to pick
and choose as in the case of place names, but their sound
values may be of almost equal importance in his choice
and disposition of them.   This applies to the study of
poetry in other languages as well as in our own, and a
student, who has hitherto thought Horace a mere dealer
in moral platitudes, may have a sudden illumination
when he becomes aware of the appeal made to his ear
by such lines as :‡

> *Cres*cen*tem* sequi*tur cur*a pe*cun*iam.
> Cæ*sar* His*pan*a *repet*it *Pen*at*e*s
> S*per*ne pu*er ne*que tu choreas
> *Ter* pede *ter*ram

There is no difficulty in finding equally striking examples
in our own poetry.

    *J. Milton—*Lycidas*, ll, 161-2, ed. Grierson, 1925.
    †*Lives of the Poets*, "Pope," World's Classics, II, p. 343.   (The couplet as
printed by J. Sutherland, *op. cit.*, *The Dunciad* (A), Bk. III, 11, 79-80.)
    ‡ These examples are given by Archibald Y. Campbell—*Horace, A New Inter-
pretation*. 1934, p. 292.

> But such a tide as moving *seems* asleep*
>   . . . *p*aste of a*p*ricots,
> And coffee *ta*bles *bot*ched with *p*earl, and li*ttl*e
>   *bea*ten *b*rassware *p*ots :† . . .

In some cases the sounds are not only beautiful, harsh or grotesque in sympathy with the feeling of the passage, but are an actual echo of the meaning, so that as Dryden says of Virgil,

> . . . verse is everywhere sounding the very thing
> in your Eares, whose sence it bears : . . .

In the last example quoted from Horace we have not only the emphatic repetition of the syllable *ter* but it comes in the triple time of the dance to which the line refers. In

> trahuntque siccas machinæ carinas

we seem to feel the jolt with which the boats move from their winter resting places, the straining of the hawsers and the grating of the keels on the shingle. In

> mare Caspium
> vexant inaequales procellæ

we hear the sounds of the wind, and in

> unde loquaces
> lymphæ desiliunt tuæ

the babbling of the stream on a summer day.‡ There is the feel of vigorous movement in :

> Push hard across the sand,
>   For the salt wind gathers breath ;¶ . . .

---

* A. Tennyson—*Crossing the Bar.*
† J. E. Flecker—*Collected Poems*, 1916, " Gates of Damascus."
‡ Horace—*Odes*, I, iv, 2 ; II, ix, 2-3 ; III, xiii, 15-16.
¶ Swinburne—*Poems and Ballads*, " A Song in Time of Order."

and the hypnotic rhythm of the march in

> Foot-foot-foot-foot-sloggin' over Africa—
> (Boots-boots-boots-boots—movin' up and down
> again !)*

In the examples quoted each word is one element in a pattern of sounds or meanings. In the same way each word is an element in a rhythmical pattern. The subject of metre is too technical to be entered upon here, but its essential paradox may be noted. Every line of verse, whether, accentual, quantitative or syllabic, is different in its rhythm from every other, yet each exemplifies the pattern of the metre in which it is written, and upon which it is a variation. To read verse that pattern must run in our heads, so that we may be conscious of each line as at once conforming to and departing from it. In this combination of conformity and variation lies our delight. The pattern may be a standard one, for example, the heroic couplet, which has served so many purposes in English. In another case it may be one peculiar to a particular poet or a particular poem. Thus Browning may almost be said to invent a new metrical form for every poem he writes. In such a case we can find out only by reading the poem itself how it must be read. In some cases we must understand a little of the theory upon which the verse is based. Thus Milton's blank verse obeys different laws from Shakespeare's. In some cases it may be helpful to hear a specimen read aloud. In no case can we read verse with the enjoyment proper to it, unless it is made audible to us, either by the lips or in our inner speech for the mind's ear.

In order to appreciate the sound of verse it is of course necessary for the student to know how to pronounce the words. Since the poet's vocabulary may be more learned

---

* Kipling—*Barrack-Room Ballads*, " Boots."

than his own, or belong to a different age and a different
educational tradition, there are real difficulties here,
even when, as in the case of Robert Burns or William
Barnes, difficulties of dialect do not come in. Misunder-
standings may be grotesque, like that of the little girl
who made two syllables of the proper name in

> Whether beyond the stormy Hebrides, . . .

and wondered what sort of curious creatures *he-brides*
might be. The beauty of

> Blind Thamyris and blind Mæonides
> And Tiresias and Phineus Prophets old :* . . .

is destroyed if we do not know that the proper names are
accented Tha′myris, Mæo′nidēs, Tire′sias, Phī′neūs,†
or that Milton's prosody prescribes the elision of the
third vowel of *Tiresias*.‡   It is nevertheless a curious
fact that verse will survive changes in pronunciation.
We do not know for certain how Shakespeare spoke :
we do know that his speech differed in important
respect from our own. In how many different ways have
schoolboys been taught in one generation and in this
country alone to pronounce

> incipe, parve puer, risu cognoscere matrem :   . .

A poet's effects may depend in part upon the use of
words which are rich and strange. In another case simple
and homely words may be used which draw their power
from the associations of everyday life. There is no word
or phrase in George Herbert's poem, *Love*, which would
need explanation to a child, yet there can be no more

---

* J. Milton—*Paradise Lost*, III, 35-36, ed. Grierson.
† Stress and quantity marks according to *The Oxford Companion to Classical Literature*.
‡ Robert Bridges—*Milton's Prosody*, 1921, p. 24.

tremendous meaning than is conveyed in its last two
lines :*

> " You must sit down " says Love, " and taste My
> meat."
> So I did sit and eat.

In the last line, in which no word has more than three
letters, is the culmination of the debate between the soul
and God, under the similitude of a kindly host putting
at ease a timid guest.

Remarkable effects may be produced by the combination of words which are unremarkable in themselves or
are rendered commonplace by familiarity and everyday
use.   Cold as flint or steel, when taken separately, they
strike sparks from one another, when brought together.
Consider A. E. Housman's line :†

> The troubles of our proud and angry dust. . .

Disregarding the particles, we have four everyday words,
troubles, *proud*, *angry* and *dust*.   The first is a petty word
by which to refer to the tragedy of human life.   It is the
word we use for our minor afflictions and for other peoples' misfortunes, when they call forth our pity, miti-
gated by a conviction that they are less serious than they
are taken to be.   It implies sympathy, but a certain
detachment, and here it seems to be used deliberately to
belittle our sense of human dignity.   *Proud* and *angry* at
once clash with *dust*.   The essence of Housman's scepticism and pessimism is concentrated in this last word
with its implication of the vanity and ridiculousness of
such passions in humanity.

All this play of thought and feeling lies within the line
itself and constitutes its meaning.   But as the word *dust*

---

* *The Poems of George Herbert*, ed. Waugh 1907.

† *Last Poems*, IX, 25.

completes the magic of the line it calls up a vast background of associations of a very different kind, caught up in its long history, which give it weight and colour. These are the echoes of other phrases which come to mind only if we pause in our reading and await their appearance —" And the Lord God formed man of the dust of the ground and breathed into his nostrils the breath of life ; and man became a living soul." " Dust as we are, the immortal spirit grows like harmony in music." ". . . . earth to earth, ashes to ashes, dust to dust ; in sure and certain hope of the Resurrection to Eternal Life." " Dust to the dust ! but the pure spirit shall flow Back to the burning fountain whence it came."* Thus the very word which is used to imply the negation of human hopes and values is bound up with the phrases in which they have been most confidently asserted, so that despair and disbelief appear as eddies in the stream of faith, from which even this expression of scepticism and pessimism draws its force.

Such an examination of verse, or of the products of any other art, depends upon the observation of a single mind. Judgments based upon it may therefore have a restricted validity, since what happens in one mind may not happen in another. There is little use in pretending to oneself that one sees beauty or wit in a passage simply because it has been praised for these qualities. We can only find them for ourselves, though we can hope to find them where others have found them before. One reader's report of his mental processes may not be true for another, but it may suggest to him how he may pursue similar inquiries for himself. This, and not the formulation of rules or the issue of judgments, is the work that the great critics do for us.

---

* *Genesis*, II, 7 ; Wordsworth—*The Prelude*, 340 ; *The Book of Common Prayer*, The Order for the Burial of the Dead " ; Shelley—*Adonais*, XXXVIII.

The good critic is he who relates the adventures of his soul among masterpieces.*

We do not read to give attention to the minutiæ of metre, vocal sounds and verbal associations, but we must read in such a way as to let them make their proper contributions to our pleasure. We may afterwards return to a passage in order to seek a closer acquaintance with it and to inquire how that pleasure has arisen. We shall not then be open to Pope's jibe at :†

> Each wight, who reads not, and but scans and spells,
> Each word-catcher that lives on syllables, . . .

Acquaintance with a great masterpiece comes slowly, and not at a first hasty reading. A professor of English literature once remarked to me that it was one of the happiest circumstances of his life that he had to read *Paradise Lost* every session with his students, as he found new beauties in it at every re-reading.

Any piece of writing implies an understanding between the writer and his immediate audience. Not only does this imply that he uses words in the senses in which his audience will understand them, but he takes for granted a mass of common knowledge of the circumstances of his time. With the passage of time this assumption very rapidly ceases to be true. Listen to a music hall comedian and consider how many of his points depend for their effect upon what must soon be forgotten. Aristophanes and Plautus, Shakespeare and W. S. Gilbert have all suffered in different degrees from this process. When for the first time the Fairy Queen sang :

> Oh, Captain Shaw !
> Type of true love kept under !

---

* Anatole France—*La Vie Litteraine*, Preface. " Le bon critique est celui qui raconte les aventures de son âme au milieu des chefs-d'œuvre."
† " Prologue to the Satires," 11, 165-6.

we can imagine how immediately the Savoy audience responded, but for a young man or woman to-day the line needs, or will very soon need, a discreet note to the effect that Captain Shaw was the head of the London Fire Brigade. In the case of older writers it has too often happened that a similar note was not written when it was still possible to supply it.

Notes are at best unsatisfactory substitutes for the power of immediately understanding an author. They are " often necessary, but they are necessary evils."* How then should we use them ?

> Let him, that is yet unacquainted with the powers of Shakespeare, and who desires to feel the highest pleasure that the drama can give, read every play, from the first scene to the last, with utter negligence of all his commentators. When his fancy is once on the wing, let it not stoop at correction or explanation. . . . Let him read on through brightness and obscurity, through integrity and corruption ; . . . And when the pleasures of novelty have ceased, let him attempt exactness, and read the commentators.
>
> Particular passages are cleared by notes, but the general effect of the work is weakened . . . the reader is weary, he suspects not why ; and at last throws away the book which he has too diligently studied.
>
> Parts are not to be examined till the whole has been surveyed ; . . . a close approach shows the smaller niceties, but the beauty of the whole is discerned no longer.*

In these sentences Johnson is addressing the readers of his own edition of Shakespeare. Here are the words of a

---

* S. Johnson—Preface to the Works of Shakespeare, 1765.

later scholar, referring to his own notes in his edition
of Horace's Odes:*

If therefore notes are to be of real use, they must be
notes, which do not merely point out what is right,
but which clearly indicate the reasons why one thing
is right and another wrong. . . . Personally I
should esteem my notes most successful if I found that
a student, after reading what I had to say on some
difficult passage, was enabled not only to disagree
with my conclusions but also to provide himself with
the weapons for successfully attacking them.

A student who reads the lines from *Paradise Lost*
quoted above, without knowing anything about
Thamyris and the rest, will gather from the lines themselves the essential fact, that, like Milton, they were
blind. A book of reference, or his editor's notes, will tell
him the story of each. To bring this information to the
forefront of consciousness (whether from the stores of
memory or from a dictionary of mythology) does little
to illumine the poetry. In fact it brings to mind points
in which the comparison is inappropriate. To come to
Paradise Lost, as the " fit audience " of Milton's own day
did, was to come with such old tales half-remembered
from youthful studies, so that they made a rich background to the ideas and images brought immediately
before consciousness. We cannot—unless we are specia-
list scholars—get ourselves a seventeenth century education in order to read Milton and a fourteenth century
education in order to read Chaucer, but we can read
Homer and Ovid, Vergil and Dante, in translations if
not in the original languages, and this will be more helpful, as well as more enjoyable, than " mugging up "
notes, which are pointers to such reading rather than
substitutes for it.

* T. E. Page—*Q. Horatii Flacci Carminum Libri IV*, 1883, Preface.

In the last resort poetry cannot be " explained."

I take up some lines of poetry and say I will explain them and make the effort, always to end in giving it up. . . . There is nothing to be done except to read out with friendliest voice the lines I started to make plain. What can be explained is not poetry.*

Definition.

A stimulus is any physical event capable of affecting a sense organ so as to initiate a nervous impulse in the sensory nerve attached to it.

---

* J. B. Yeats—*Passages from the Letters*, selected by E. Pound, 1917.

CHAPTER XII

READING

> . . . some books are to be read only in parts; others to be read, but not curiously; and some few to be read wholly, and with diligence and attention.

> A man ought to read just as inclination leads him; for what he reads as a task will do him little good.

> "What, have you not read it through?"
> "No, Sir, do *you* read books *through*?"

The purpose of reading is to obtain from the printed page the information, the thoughts or the feelings which the writer sought to convey to his readers. There may be a further purpose—to analyse, to select, to criticise, to enjoy—but that further purpose requires that we first discover what the author's meaning is.

In school reading has too often meant reading aloud. To be able to read aloud in an acceptable way is a useful social accomplishment; silent reading is an everyday necessity. The schools probably emphasised reading aloud because of the supposed difficulty of teaching silent reading: Johnnie, left with a book, might day-dream instead of reading it; Johnnie, reading aloud, was under control; and so were the class, who must hang on Johnnie's lips or risk execution for not knowing the place. And at intervals, during this futile and exasperating procedure, Jimmie or Willie would be found with a "blood" under the desk and suffer condign punishment.

Note.—The quotations at the head of the Chapter are from Francis Bacon—*Essayes or Counsels, Civil & Morall,* "Of Studies," Everyman's Library; *Boswell's Life of Johnson, ed cit.,* I, 428; *ibid.,* II. 226.

It was probably this system which produced so many slow readers. If the purpose of reading is to get the author's meaning from the printed page in the most efficient way possible, it was Jimmie and Willie with their " bloods " who were learning to read—they wanted the meaning, they were getting it, and they were constantly gaining skill in getting it more efficiently. Johnnie was mainly anxious to stumble through his paragraph and sit down : there can be no incentive to good oral reading, when your audience has no desire to listen to you. As for the more virtuous part of the audience, who had not provided themselves with more engrossing reading matter, they alternated between attending to the words of the reader and reading ahead of him, or daydreaming. This situation was still further aggravated when, the day's assignment having been read through, the next boy was sent back to the beginning, and the whole thing had to be suffered again.

There is nothing specially " modern " in the view that Jimmie and Willie were on the right track. So old and respectable an authority as Dr. Johnson shared it.

> I am always for getting a boy forward in his learning ; for that is a sure good. I would let him at first read *any* English book which happens to engage his attention ; because you have done a great deal when you have brought him to have entertainment from a book.*

Matters might however be improved by providing better material than the " blood," as regards print and paper, and possibly content, though the last is less certain, if we remember G. K. Chesterton's essay in defence of penny dreadfuls, or reflect that the book studied in this tedious fashion to-day may be *Treasure Island*, which an

---

* *Ibid*, III, p. 385.

earlier generation risked punishment to read surreptitiously.

Why was this procedure so unfortunate in its results ? To learn an activity, the learner must practise the activity itself. In this case the activity is getting the meaning from the printed page. To practise it you must be unaware of the meaning, desirous of getting it and free to get it in your own quickest time. Reading aloud is limited by the speed at which our vocal organs produce speech sounds, and an ordinary rate of speech is about one hundred and twenty words per minute. Silent reading is limited only by the rate at which our minds can grasp the meaning of the lines of print, and one hundred and twenty words per minute is a very slow rate for silent reading, except in special circumstances to which we shall return. According to Professor Starch the average rate of silent reading in the 3rd Grade is 2.1 words per second, which is more than one hundred and twenty words per minute ; and in the 8th Grade it is 4.0 words per second or two hundred and forty words per minute.* It must be remembered that, as these figures are averages, half the class will be capable of reading more rapidly. Thus the boy who is reading aloud is not likely to be improving his rate of reading ; and his hearers, if like good children they are following on the printed page, are actually establishing bad reading habits instead of increasing their skill.

Let us see in what good reading habits consist. Reading is based upon speech. Some thought or feeling arises in the speaker's mind which he wishes to communicate. He expresses it in words. These words, when heard by

---

* Children in the 3rd Grade will mostly be about 8, and children in the 8th Grade about 13 years old.

the person addressed, arouse in *his* mind a meaning sufficiently similar to that in the mind of the speaker to serve his purpose. These links between thought and word, which give rise to speech, and between word and thought, which give rise to meaning, are established in infancy and so precede the child's first steps in learning to read. By slow and painful processes, upon which we need not enter here, a writer's thoughts make their way into print. Then begins the second part of the process of communication by printed or written symbol, that which we call reading. The learner approaches the printed symbol equipped with his speech habits. Words have meanings in his mind, but for him words are spoken words—groups of speech sounds or movements of his vocal organs made in pronouncing them, or both. The printed symbols are representations—even in the case of our unreformed orthography—of the sounds of the words, and so the obvious first step is to learn to associate the printed word with the spoken word by pronouncing the word as the eye falls upon the letters that stand for it. There is thus established the sequence :

printed symbol → speech movements → sound → meaning

It is quite evident that the speech movements are unnecessary—in listening to spoken language we do not make over again the movements required to produce it. A moment's consideration will show that the speech sounds are equally unnecessary. Why should not we go as directly from the printed word to its meaning as from the spoken word to its meaning ? Because we are slow to relinquish a habit once learned and because, unless we read a great deal, the spoken word is more familiar to us than its printed symbol. The old sequence does not, however, go on unmodified. We cease to make the sounds of the words aloud, as we do not wish to disturb others or to draw attention to ourselves. An unpractised reader can, however, be observed to make the movements of lips and tongue which form the words ; and in more practised readers, though these movements may not be visible, they may still be present in some degree. The longer we practise any activity the more we tend to drop out unnecessary elements in it—that is a process which we noted in describing how a piece of skill is learned. The same happens here. The more we read, especially if we read in an active, pur-posive way intent on getting at the writer's meaning, the more these movements drop out. The same thing happens with the mental representation of the sounds of the words, which we may continue to hear as a kind of inner speech, when the vocal movements have dropped out. These too may become less prominent and dis-appear.*

To someone who reads only to amuse himself, his rate of reading may be unimportant. Why should he not read at the rate that suits him, just as he walks at the rate that suits him when he takes the air ? For the student it is another matter. His power of reading is one of his essential tools and, for him, to be unable to read reasonably quickly is to be seriously handicapped.

It is a handicap which is not uncommon. Rates of reading vary greatly, even among students who have successfully taken their degrees at a university. The following table shows the reading speeds of 419 of the writer's students, including 241 graduates and 178 non-graduates.

---

* St. Augustine mentions as worthy of remark that, when St Ambrose was reading, " his eye glided over the pages, . . . but his voice and tongue were at rest." *Confessions*, Ch. VI, tr. Pusey.

Words per minute	Number of students
850—899	2
800—849	—
750—799	—
700—749	3
650—699	—
600—649	5
550—599	16
500—549	31
450—499	68
400—449	89
350—399	82
300—349	70
250—299	38
200—249	15
	419

The striking fact about these figures is their diversity. The two fastest readers, both graduate students, read three and a half time as fast as the slowest graduate student and more than four times as fast as the slowest non-graduate student. It may be thought that the slow readers grasp and retain more of what they read than do the fast ones. This is not found to be the case. In general the fast readers understand and remember more of what they read. This is not the paradox that it may at first sight appear, for the slower readers are hampered all the time by the comparative inefficiency of their reading machinery, mental and physical. It should be noted in this connection that, when tests, such as this, are given to measure speed of reading, easy material is used, which does not make it necessary to go slow in order to grasp its meaning. The reader, who can get along with such material at over eight hundred and fifty words per minute, does not always read at this speed, any more than a driver, whose car can do eighty miles an hour takes road-crossings, villages, bridges and corners at this speed. He uses the speed suitable to the occasion. Nevertheless the driver of a vehicle which can scarcely exceed twenty miles an hour will not reach a desired destination with either the same expedition or the same comfort. The fast reader has it within his power to pass quickly over what does not need study and to give some of the time so saved to a closer examination of the passages that require it, to re-reading, and to other methods of study.

Every student will find it worth while to know his reading speed. He need only choose a passage that is not familiar to him, but is of a kind to which he is accustomed, which is clearly printed, and which presents no difficulties of unusual language or ideas beyond his everyday range of thought. It should not be controversial, lest either his disagreement or his enthusiastic acceptance should make him pause. Easy narrative is usually the best material. He should get a friend to time him, by giving him a signal to begin and stopping him after one minute. He should aim at reading as quickly as he would do when reading a novel for pleasure. He should then compare his speed with the figures given in the table on p. 188. Whatever speed he finds in this way, it is probable that he can improve it by giving attention to his reading habits, and this may be well worth while, unless he is already one of the fast readers. If his rate is below three hundred words per minute, he may be advised to go to some trouble to increase it.

An important factor in speed of reading is the kind of movements made by the eyes in following the lines of print. These movements depend upon habits formed in

the early stages of learning to read and are largely
determined by the methods of teaching employed. To
teach a child to read is a highly responsible undertaking,
requiring a high degree of professional skill and knowledge ; and the belief that it can be safely entrusted to
any young girl or old lady is a mistaken one, and results
in the large proportion of inefficient readers shown in
the table.

In reading as in glancing along any horizontal line—
say, the picture rail or the cornice of the room you are
sitting in—you feel as if your eyes make a continuous
movement along each line of print. It is not so. Hold
a mirror so that you can see in it the reflection of someone's eyes, while you look over his shoulder and he reads
a paragraph in a book. You can easily distinguish the
movement to the right which follows each line of print,
and the sweeping movement to the left which takes the
eyes back to the beginning of the next line. The movement to the right is not continuous. You will count some
three, four or five movements, with short pauses between
them. The reading is done during the pauses. The
movements are too rapid for the print to be seen as
anything but a blur, and last too short a time to be
noticeable to the reader.

These movements have been recorded in a number of
ingenious ways. The most recently invented apparatus
is one which photographs two small rays of light reflected
from the surface of the subject's eyes, as he looks into
the eye-piece of the apparatus and reads the line of
print exposed in it. The record shows how many times
his eyes pause for each line, the length of each pause, and
the direction of each movement.

When we look straight in front with both eyes open,
our field of vision includes about 140°. Looking with
one eye it is about 90°. Until we test the matter we do

not notice that the whole of this field is not equally clear. This is partly because, as soon as we have reason to be interested in any one part of the field, our eyes immediately turn so as to bring it into the area of clearest vision, if it is not there already, and because, our eyes making frequent flitting movements throughout the field, our perceptual processes " fill in " what is not actually in the area of clear vision at the moment. Thus we do not notice that objects near the boundary of the field are seen without colour, that those a little nearer in are still seen as uncoloured, if they happen to be green or red. This can easily be observed by covering one eye, fixing the other upon a mark directly in front, say on a large sheet of paper fixed to the wall, and getting a friend to introduce small pieces of coloured paper into the field of vision from the side, marking the point at which each becomes visible and the point at which its colour is perceived. The subject's face must be brought close to the wall. The pieces of paper should be mounted on a convenient holder—for example, a wooden pen-holder split at the end to grip them.

The area of clear vision can be found by introducing in the same way single letters cut from a newspaper or made neatly with a pen. It will then be found that the area within which they can be read is restricted. Its actual size will of course depend upon the distance at which the paper is held from the eye. It corresponds to the area of the retina called the *fovea* or yellow spot.

At each pause we perceive only the words which fall within the area of clear vision, the eye moves on, another portion of the line is made visible, and so a perception of the line of print is built up. The groups of words so perceived are not necessarily either grammatical units or meaningful units. As we have seen (p. 65) the contribution made to the meaning of a sentence by a particular word may not be determined until the end of the sentence is reached. The successive " eyefuls " of print must therefore be put together before they yield their meaning : they do not give a succession of independent units of meaning. The order in which the successive " eyefuls " are taken is thus less important than it at first seems. Now at each pause the area of clear vision includes parts of the lines of print immediately above and immediately below that to which the eyes are directed. It is therefore possible to read three or more lines of print in the course of each movement of the eyes to the right. The separate pieces are not taken in the order in which they were written down and, since it is not necessary to follow this order, the next three lines may be read while the eyes are moving to the left. It is in this way that high reading speeds are attained. At these speeds there can be little or no reproduction of the movements of the vocal organs and little or no inner speech. Such rapid reading is therefore inappropriate when these are required for appreciation of the material being studied.

There are in fact no disadvantages in being a fast reader—unless it be the danger of a possible shortage of reading matter. The convalescent who requires four novels a day—in addition to *The Times*, *Bradshaw*, Patience cards and such serious reading matter as he may have in hand—may be a trouble to those who have to keep him supplied, but he would not seem to be a loser himself.

We do not see individual letters as we read. We recognise words by their general shape, together with the context. Thus misspellings do not usually catch our attention unless we are looking for them—say in correcting proofs—and then they may prove elusive. We may even pass over a wrong word, reading in place of it the one which makes sense, without noticing the error. Fast readers are, of course, more likely to do this than slow ones, who are nearer to schoolroom methods of reading. Modern teaching encourages the child to recognise words as wholes, instead of deciphering them letter by letter and this produces more skilful readers.

We may not even see the individual words as we read, except for the important ones, but take whole phrases as our units. Thus the little words that occur over and over again are scarcely seen. More than twenty years ago Hilaire Belloc published an essay on the word " And." Having shown how many subtle uses it can be put to, he concluded his essay by remarking that the word was " not really necessary at all," and that he had not brought it once into his own sentences in the essay. Curiosity made me re-read the essay to see. I found a few " ands." I read it again and found a few more. I went through it line by line, not reading, but looking at each word. I got some more. Finally, to bring the matter to a conclusion, I began at the end of the essay, and scanned each line backwards, inspecting each word. There were more. When Belloc republished this essay in the volume " On," I looked to see how many of his " ands " had been noted. Most of them had been removed, but seven remained.

A student scarcely needs to be told to take care of his microscope or his slide-rule. These necessary instruments will clearly lose their usefulness if they are misused. Yet he will frequently misuse his eyes, which are of more importance to him and which cannot be replaced. There have been great scholars who have overcome serious physical defects, but there is no need to court such handicaps.

A good light is the first need. It should be neither too bright—direct sunlight, for example—nor too dull.

The page upon which the eyes are turned should be the brightest part of the field of vision. Otherwise a conflict is set up—the bright light coming from beyond the book stimulates the mechanism of the eye to close the pupil and admit less light, while the comparative dimness of the page stimulates the opposite response, and there is a consequent feeling of strain. The reader should therefore sit so that the source of light is behind him, but so that his own shadow does not fall on the page. The page should be evenly lit. When making notes from a book, both book and writing paper should be similarly lit. Otherwise the eyes have to re-adapt themselves every time they move from the one to the other. This happens when copying in the lecture room from a black-board, and it has been shown that there is a definite advantage, from the point of view of the pupil or student, in substituting a light-coloured surface and a dark blue chalk.

The best light is daylight. Flickering lights are the most harmful. Electricity gives the best artificial light. Nowadays it is usually quite steady. Current alternating at a rate which gives a visible flicker should be avoided. Gas and oil are liable to give a flickering light. They also use up oxygen, give out waste products of combustion and make the air humid and warm. Many headaches attributed to study have nothing to do with mental activity, but are directly due to a stuffy atmosphere, and can be prevented by avoiding such conditions. An electric torch, used for reading, is likely to illuminate the page unevenly. The best artificial lighting is indirect, diffused electric lighting.

Reading, writing, sewing, handwork, dissection and drawing are performed close to the eyes. They therefore necessitate *accommodation*, the alteration in the curvature of the lens of the eye which enables us to focus objects at different distances. The lens of the eye is not a rigid body, like a lens of glass, and accommodation is brought about by a muscular pull upon it, which, like any other exertion of muscular force is fatiguing, if maintained for a long time. The periods of such work should therefore be limited, and interspersed if possible with activities which give these muscles a rest. Fine work should be done as far as possible in daylight and, if possible, early in the day.

Eye defects, if not detected, may lead to serious trouble. It is a pity that this should be allowed to happen as many of them can be corrected, and most of them alleviated. It is therefore wise to consult an oculist, even if there is no evidence of immediate need to do so. Gross defects of vision may go unsuspected—someone with short sight, for instance, never having seen the world through a normal pair of eyes, may be quite unaware of the difficulties under which he labours—and slight defects, such as will pass unnoted at a routine medical inspection, may give rise to cumulative effects of a serious nature over a period of years.

The position of the page in relation to the eyes is also of importance. The line of print should be parallel to the line which joins the centres of the two eyes. Otherwise the movement of following the lines of print is unnecessarily complicated and unnecessarily fatiguing. The page should be at right-angles to the line of sight, since otherwise (that is, if the page be tilted back or forward, or to one side) the apparent size of the letters will be diminished along one dimension.

Less important than the art of reading is the art of listening. There has always been the lecture, as an important method of instruction, and to-day the radio reaches everyone with a variety of talks on all possible subjects.

The great difference between reading and listening is

that the reader can go at his own pace, whereas the listener must accommodate himself to the pace of the lecturer—except in so far as it may be possible on occasion to stop him in order to ask a question. In this the advantage is on the side of the reader, who can put down the book to consult a dictionary or an atlas, re-read a passage that is not clear at first sight, follow up his own train of thought, that something in his book has started, or give himself a breather. The listener must maintain a continuous attention, and this may be difficult, unless the lecture happens to be very exactly adjusted to his particular needs—his knowledge of the subject and his quickness of mind.

We are much less able to maintain such a continuous attention than we usually believe. If the reader will place a watch on a table, and gradually withdraw from it to the point at which he can just hear its ticking, he will find that its ticking appears to him to be intermittent. He hears it, and then he cannot hear it, and then he hears it again. This is not because the ticking of the watch varies in loudness (though it will be necessary to exclude variations in background noise which may make it appear to do so) but because his attention to it varies in spite of all efforts to keep it constant. Thus the sound appears to vary for the same reason that makes possible a changed view of the reversible perspective figure (p. 55). It is not surprising that we miss parts of a lecture that puts a strain on the attention.

A good lecturer allows for these difficulties on the part of the listener. As to pace, he must compromise. He may not adopt the principle implied in the army maxim that the pace of the regiment is the pace of the man with the shortest legs, but he must approximate to it. He will also, if he is skilful, allow for the inevitable strain upon his audience's attention by reducing the effort

necessary at intervals—by varying his pace, by suitable
pauses, by supplying a sufficient number of illustrations,
by an occasional good story, relevant if possible, by the
use of paradox to draw attention to a critical point that
might otherwise be missed, by explaining at the beginning
what ground he intends to cover, by making clear his
progress through this sequence as each stage is passed,
by summarising his argument as he goes along, and,
generally, by keeping in touch with his audience and
helping them over difficulties as these present themselves.
In so far as the lecturer can do this the lecture has some
advantages over reading. It is intermediate between cold
print and individual contact with a tutor. Something
of the personal enthusiasm and temperament of the
lecturer gets into a lecture, which cannot get into a book.
To this extent the advantage is on the side of the lecture.

A lecture differs from a lesson in that the responsibility
of the lecturer is discharged when he has set out for his
audience in a suitable manner the material that it is his
business to put before them. The teacher's responsibility
does not end there, for, though a lecture has been de-
livered even if no one has listened to it, a lesson has not
been taught unless it has been learned. A student may
nevertheless be justified in thinking that a lecturer has
not properly performed his office, if he has merely written
out his matter, very much as if he were preparing it for
the printer, and then read it aloud at a steady pace and
in a monotonous voice. It is very difficult to learn
anything from this kind of lecturing, for it makes the
worst of both worlds—there is neither the advantage of
personal contact nor the opportunity to assimilate the
material at one's own pace, and, in the worst cases, much
may be lost because it is actually inaudible. It would
be much more satisfactory to circulate the material in
typescript.

Cheap and handy methods of reproducing verbal matter have in fact gone far to put the lecture out of date as a method of teaching. As a method of conveying information it is clumsy and uncertain, and the text-book or the mimeographed summary should take the place of laborious and often inaccurate or defective notes. On the other hand, the lecture, properly used, is stimulating as no text-book is likely to be, and it can apply its stimulus at the exact point where it is needed—the difficulty which the student may find discouraging when he meets it in solitude. It is also social. Reading is a solitary occupation. A topic which comes up in a lecture may call forth a response which makes the class aware as a body of their approval or dissent, or of a division of opinion among them. The lecture is also a corrective to excessive dependence on the eye. Words met only in print may be only half known, and curious misconceptions may result.

I have known a student who had met the word *monoideism* only in print speak of *mon-oid'-e-ism*, which could scarcely have happened had it been heard as *mon'o-ide'ism*, a five-syllable compound of *mono* and *idea*, meaning a condition of the mind, in which it is dominated by one idea. Another type of error results when a word is met with only in a lecture and never seen in print. I have had *duck* for *duct* in examination scripts, and one student, in answer to a question on the *three-track* system of school organisation, whereby the dull, the average, and the able are allowed to proceed with their work in parallel classes at appropriate speeds, referred to as the *free-tract* system. A word is a seen as well as a heard entity, and should be known in both ways.

Very different rates of reading are appropriate to different kinds of material. The rate depends upon the speed at which the reader can reconstruct the author's meaning, and assimilate or criticise it, according to his purpose. Thus different rates may also be appropriate to different readers in the case of the same material.

Literature probably provides the extremes of material appropriate to high or to low speeds of reading. The lyric, in which the weight of every syllable must be allowed for, in which the clashes and harmonies of the speech sounds must be listened for, in which each word carries a complex meaning, including an indefinite background of suggestion, and in which all these factors have to come together into a subtle unity, does not give up its secret at the first quick glance. Since the sounds of the words to the ear, and their feel to the tongue and the lips, are of the highest importance, it must be read at the rate at which it should be spoken, and this will vary from that of the most deliberate speech to that of the patter song. Thus the last line of one of Mr. Walter de la Mare's poems*

> The sweet cheat gone.

seems to need a slowness of movement beyond that possible to the voice, and audible only to the inner ear: At the other extreme we have such lingual gymnastics as the Lord Chancellor's song in *Iolanthe*.†

> When you're lying awake with a dismal headache, and repose is taboo'd by anxiety,
> I conceive you may use any language you choose to indulge in without impropriety ; . . .

Variations of pace passing almost from one of these extremes to the other may be found within a single poem.

At the other extreme is narrative, especially prose narrative. Verse must go at a speed at which it could be read aloud, since otherwise there is no point in writing

---

* " The Ghost " in *Motley and Other Poems*.
† Sir W. S. Gilbert—*The Savoy Operas*.

in metre at all.   But verse narrative, as Mr. C. S. Lewis points out* reveals its qualities, not to the close study that is wanted by the lyric, but to continuous reading, which does not linger over the turn of a phrase or the melody of a line.   Thus the effect of *Paradise Lost* is built up paragraph by paragraph, and that poem should be read so as to produce in the mind a sense of its vast spaces, great forces, mighty issues and background of illimitable time.   *Paradise Lost* can also be read in detail. Not so some other long poems.   Thus William Morris's *Story of Sigurd the Volsung,* if read with the rapidity that its easy metre makes possible, builds up an impressive cumulative effect, but this seems to be the only way to read it.

Drama may need as slow a speed of reading as lyric, but the reason may be different.   The speeches of the characters are composed, not to be read in the study, but to be spoken, and to be heard.   There is more than this to be done in producing a private performance of a play in the theatre of the mind; for the reader must be at once producer, designer of the *décor,* stage manager and all the actors.   In other words he must supply not only the words, which in the theatre would come to his ear, but all that would come to him through the eye.   While he is reading the words spoken by one of the persons of the drama, he must be conscious of each of the other persons then on the stage and the effect of these words upon them.   In the theatre all this would be made evident to him by movement or pose ; in the study it must be supplied by his own imagination.   Frequently, too, point is given to an actor's words by the action which accompanies them.

The appropriate rate of reading may vary widely within the same scientific or philosophical work.   An

*C. S. Lewis—*A Preface to Milton.*

argument may turn upon a definition or statement of a principle which must be closely studied—which must in fact be examined word by word, like a legal document. To fail to treat it in this way may be to miss the point of what follows, and so the reader who has not learned to vary his speed may find himself in difficulties.

This is specially striking in mathematics. Mathematical symbols permit of very condensed statement. That is their use. The reader who expects to pass down the page at the same speed when he passes from a statement in words to a statement in symbols will experience a feeling of frustration, and he may interpret this as a sign of his unfitness for mathematics, when it is only a sign that his reading habits need modification. A symbolic statement must be deciphered rather than read. Each symbol must be separately considered, and its part in the whole made out. This is reflected in the different eye-movements involved. In reading print, as we have seen, the eyes move along the lines, and return movements are the marks of the inexpert reader. In reading a mathematical formula the eyes make exploratory movements in this direction and in that, until the whole is known.

The rate of reading may be determined not by the nature of the material but by the purpose in view in reading it. If the purpose is skipping or skimming, then the rate will vary from the fastest rate at which the reader can deal with print, to the most patient scrutiny of the things he is looking for, when he finds them. Skipping is the art of passing over what is not to our purpose. There is much, for example, in Boswell's *Johnson* that need not detain the ordinary reader. Our older novelists supply lengthy moral disquisitions and descriptions, that were more to the tastes of their contemporaries than to ours. Some of their stories were produced as serials, and in a leisurely way rehearse at intervals what the reader has learned already, no doubt because the author has in mind a reader who has started in the middle of the tale. Judicious skipping makes it possible to enjoy great works of character and imagination, which we should otherwise neglect.

Skimming is rather the art of getting from a book what we happen to want, when it is not what the author in the main intended to give. With some special interest in view, we approach a number of writers to see what information they give on a particular topic, or what views they hold on a particular subject. Thus a historian, interested in some one aspect of domestic life, might search all the diaries, letters and memoirs of a particular country and period for matter bearing upon it. He would come on much fascinating matter connected with other subjects, which would tend to delay him by the way, but his serious purpose would be hindered by letting it side-track him. Such treatment, however fitting for the diarist and letter-writer, might seem unfitted to the dignity of the poet or philosopher. On the contrary, it is surprising how much a writer may gain by it. He is seen from a fresh point of view. He is approached with a new and vital interest. Some of his special characteristics are thrown into sharp relief. He stands up to this special test and one-sided mode of appraisement or, on the other hand, an unsuspected weakness is brought to light.

The art of skimming is closely related to the art of casual reading. Samuel Johnson, having come into his host's library, " ran eagerly to one side of the room, intent on poring over the backs of the books,"* and justified this with the explanation that :

When we inquire into any subject, the first thing we have to do is to know what books have treated of it.

* Boswell—*ed. cit.*, II, 364-5.

This leads us to look at catalogues and the backs of books in libraries.

This is the great justification of the open shelf system in libraries, and the pleasant habit of wandering round the shelves in the bookseller's shop. The advantages are still greater if we may look inside. It is extraordinary how often, in handling a book in this casual fashion, one's eye is caught by a passage relevant to a subject in which one is specially interested—sometimes, as a subsequent careful reading may show, the only such passage in it.

Such casual reading has a particular value in that it may afford some insight into other departments of study besides one's own. There is a distinct danger in limiting oneself to a narrow range of subject matter. It would be difficult to name two subjects of study which are entirely unconnected either in their subject matter, their principles or their methods. The separation of the departments of science and scholarship is a matter of convenience only. It sometimes gives the student a false impression. This begins in school. A class may express surprise on being asked to take out their atlases for a history lesson, sharing the view expressed in the couplet :*

> Geography is about Maps,
> But History is about Chaps.

From the point of view of both interest and usefulness, the student can hardly read too widely, and there is to-day no lack of cheap and authoritative " popularisers " which afford an easy approach to almost every department of knowledge.

At the opposite pole from the populariser is the periodical literature of a science—the articles to be found in the special journals, in which those doing research

---

* Misquoted from E. Clerihew—*Biography for Beginners.* See p. 147 *supra.* The second line should read " But Biography is . . ."

work set forth the results of their investigations for their fellow scientists. This literature represents the growing points of the science. As such it is written by specialists for specialists. This kind of writing has a form and an etiquette of its own. An article begins with a summary of the investigations or theories already published upon its subject. It goes on to define the particular problem to be dealt with—a question hitherto undetermined, a method open to criticism, a theory which is to be modified, given fresh support or disproved. The scope and method of the writer's own investigation are then described. The course taken by the investigation and the results obtained are set forth in detail. These results are then discussed, and such conclusions drawn from them as they admit of. Lastly, the contents of the article may be summarised.

How is such material to be treated ? It may be overwhelming in amount. It may require the most advanced technical knowledge. It may be spread over many different journals, published in different countries and in different languages. One issue of a journal may have articles on many unrelated topics, and one topic may have to be followed up in a number of different journals.

The method of study depends upon the purpose in view. The research worker—who has long outgrown any help that this book could give him—is concerned to read everything that bears upon his own line of work. It is primarily for him that this literature is produced. He must know exactly what has been done, and how, and with what results, if he is not to waste time in doing what has been done already. There is probably an annual publication in his science—an *index*—in which all the articles published in all the journals of his science are summarised, in such a way as to show him which are relevant to his own work and must be read.

The student may have either of two purposes in view. He may want to know the latest work on particular topics, in which case such an index will direct him to it. Or he may want to have a general acquaintance with what is being done in his science. It is a very useful practice to set aside a regular period to visit the periodical room in the library, and go through the current numbers of the journals there. There should be no attempt to read them through. Each article is written to provide all the information required by the man who is to carry this particular investigation one step further. It is therefore likely to be a more detailed account than is required by anyone else. First, then the titles of the articles should be looked at to find which are of special interest. Then in each of these the opening summary should be read, and the preliminary account of the writer's investigation. His results should then be looked at, and his conclusions. The reader is then in a position to judge whether or not he should go through the body of the article.

NOTE

In connection with the statement on p. 192 that we commonly read words without attending to the letters of which they are composed, the reader may be informed that a word which occurs frequently throughout this book has been spelt sometimes in one way and sometimes in another. Has he noticed it?

CHAPTER XIII

TRICKS OF THE TRADE

When you go into your study . . . you must bring your body along, and the problem is how to deal with it during the study period. The least you can do, one would think, is to . . . offer it a chair. But not everyone is of this opinion.

Set in a note-book, learn'd, and conn'd by rote, . . .

. . . I never took the smallest pains with my style, . . . I have, however, taken all the pains that I had patience to endure in the improvement of my handwriting. . . .

The student works with his mind rather than with his body, but even in the most abstract studies his body and the physical conditions of his work are important. The human body was evolved under primitive conditions of activity and exposure to the elements. A sedentary, indoor life is to that extent not natural to us, and our bodies show different degrees of tolerance for indoor conditions of ventilation, temperature and lighting, and for deprivation of fresh air, sunlight and exercise.

On the other hand these artificial conditions—shelter, segregation, regulated temperature, the arm-chair, the desk and the mid-night oil—are necessary conditions of mental work. Tolstoi, determined to put luxury from him and live like a peasant, did so with one reservation.

One thing I cannot do without : I must have a quiet room to work in.*

Such amenities are comparatively recent elements in

Note.—The quotations at the head of the chapter are from : Sir John Adams—*The Student's Guide*, 1938, p. 98 ; Wm. Shakespeare—*Julius Caesar*, IV, iii, 96 ; Samuel Butler—*Note-books*, 1918, p. 187.
*A. Maude—*Life of Tolstoi*, II, p. 528.

human history, and scholarship and science may almost be said to have developed with them. Privacy, glass windows, artificial lighting, internal heating, paper, printing, our writing materials, the form of our books, microscopes, typewriters, our chairs and tables, filing systems, books of reference, slide-rules, photostats and more specialised equipment are either modern inventions or, if known in ancient civilisations, passed out of use in successive periods of cultural decline. The Romans had hypocausts for heating. Hugh Capet in the tenth century had one set of glass windows which he carried from castle to castle. Until the invention of printing, books were so rare that the student normally travelled to the book, not the book to the student, and oral exposition took the place now occupied by written commentary. The slate has only recently disappeared from the schoolroom. The nineteenth century student might ruin his eyesight reading by firelight or a tallow dip.

Graham Wallas* traces the development of scientific and philosophical thought from warm countries, where " men seem to have thought most successfully in the open air, during the cool hours which follow sunset in a hot climate " ; and later, and further north, in " permanent shaded places, temple porticoes, or still later the Academe or the Stoa " ; and then in North Europe, in " the monastery cell . . ., dry and quiet, but in winter abominably cold " ; before we come to " pleasant [Tudor] rooms with their big glazed windows and open fireplaces," and the eighteenth century country house, where even " a girl below the rank of noblewoman " might meet with the indulgence of " a fire in the East Room " for solitary studies.† These developments affected only a minority, the professional scholars and

*The Great Society, 1919, pp. 183-4.
†Jane Austen—Mansfield Park.

the well-to-do : and we may still hear of an artisan student who " in order to get a time when the house was quiet for working in, went to bed at seven, got up at midnight, worked for two hours, and then went to bed again."*

Bringing our bodies with us, we bring our nervous systems, and therefore our reflex organisation. We noted in an earlier chapter that it may take an effort of will to start upon a habitual activity such as shaving or digging the garden, but that, once the activity has begun, it seems to go on more or less of itself. We can make use of this. To put down a novel, or leave a pleasant conversation, and get to work may be irksome at the moment ; but there is no reason why it should continue to be so, if we have accustomed ourselves to sit down at a certain time, or in a certain place, to certain activities. Our subordinate motor centres have learned their lesson, and, once we find ourselves in the chair or at the desk where we usually work, mind and body adopt of themselves the appropriate " set " and our thoughts flow naturally in the appropriate direction. Unfortunately it works in two ways. Having accustomed yourself to a certain chair, position of the light, pen, size of paper, height of desk or the like, you may be at a loss, when one of these conditions fails you. Your case is then like that of the schoolboy at the top of his class who, when seeking the answer to one of the teacher's questions, habitually fingered a button on his jacket, and lost his place, when one of his rivals cut it off, and his fingers sought it in vain.

A regular work place may excite a disposition to work in a very useful way. The effort of will that gets us there is only a small one and, when it has been made, we are away from the distractions which compete for our

---

* *Board of Education Special Reports* No. 2 q. in Wallas, *op. cit.*, p. 184.

attention elsewhere. It is therefore better to separate the place where one performs those routine operations that make the greatest call upon punctuality, regularity, patience, perseverance and doggedness, from the place in which one relaxes, or carries on more spontaneous activities. To enter the workroom, or sit at one's desk, is then to induce the appropriate mental set, and to be relatively free from wandering thoughts and contrary impulses, till the job in hand is completed. Work which is of absorbing interest can be done anywhere. Its own momentum will keep it going. There is no fear of going to sleep over it in an easy-chair. In fact you can continue it for longer in an easy-chair, for your muscles will not tire so quickly and demand a change of position.

To read steadily through a single book requires only a comfortable chair and a suitable light. To study in a more active manner, it may be necessary to use two or more books together, to make notes, to turn for help to books of reference. This usually means a desk or table. It should be so arranged that it is properly lighted, both during the hours of daylight and after dark. This may need a little contrivance, but it is well worth while. If it is not secured, the student finds that he " works best in the day time " or that he " works best at night," and assumes that he is the victim of some deep lying trait of character, when all that is wanted is to turn his desk round sixty degrees or buy a lamp-holder and a couple of yards of flex, so that at any hour he may have a light coming from his left. Physical circumstances and habits of mind are intimately connected. If at one time in his life the student has had to work in the late evening, because only then could he get a fire and a quiet room, he may find it difficult to work in the morning at a later time in his life, when circumstances make this possible. To recognise how the disability has arisen, is to see that it can be altered, and how to alter it.

The table should be of a suitable height. This turns upon two factors, a man's height and the distance at which his eyes focus comfortably. It should permit an easy posture of the body, in which both arms are free to manipulate, or reach for, books or papers, and neither breathing nor circulation are interfered with.

It is possible to read a book and make notes from it in an arm-chair. The ideal is no doubt one of those chairs which have a support for a book, and a little swinging ledge to write upon. A satisfactory substitute may be found in a piece of three-ply a little larger than the paper to be used, and a dozen sheets fastened to it at the top with a spring paper clip. If two sheets of cardboard pinned together at the left-hand side with brass paper fasteners are used instead, the notes made can be disposed of by placing them between the sheets of cardboard, until they are wanted for filing or study. A music stand, such as is used by a violinist, serves very well as a support for a book.

The student like a good workman should have his tools within reach. Whether you work in an easy-chair or at a desk, the books that you are most likely to want should be so placed that you can put your hand upon them without leaving your seat. The fact that you can do this may make all the difference between verifying a point of pronunciation, derivation, grammar, the date of an event, the location of a place, and failing to do so, because the book is on the other side of the room or upstairs, and you can look it up next time you have to get up anyhow. Either you forget, or you lose interest, or you look it up in a perfunctory manner which does not fix the matter for you, or you continue to vacillate between one view and the other, so that, when you do

look it up, you have already established a lasting un-
certainty in your mind that cannot be easily removed.

In making notes from books we may have very
different purposes in view on different occasions. The
simplest kind of note is a quotation—an isolated passage
is interesting and worth preserving, or we want to quote
it somewhere, and we copy it out.

On another occasion, perhaps with a different kind of
book, the note-making may be part of the process of
understanding the book. It would seem at first sight
that the student, a novice at the subject, can scarcely
hope, in a hasty scribble, to improve upon the way in
which the author has set out his subject matter, of which
he is a master. There are two answers to this. The book
was not written specially for you, and your own notes
may therefore serve your particular needs better ; and,
secondly, the note-making is part of the activity by
which you get a grasp of the subject matter of the book :
it is not so much the notes that are of value (they may
on some occasions go into the waste-paper basket without
being looked at) but the fact of having made them.

Notes made for subsequent use include notes made
from borrowed books. Such notes are a substitute for
putting the book on one's own shelves for future reference.
When the book is one's own and therefore still available,
the notes may be useful for reference in future, for they
may summarise a lengthy argument, so that, by looking
through them, one has the heads of it with a minimum of
trouble. Again they may translate the author's statements into a terminology more familiar to oneself—an
article in a foreign journal may sometimes be more
conveniently summarised in one's own language than in
that in which it is written, if one does not readily think
in the latter. In such a case, it may be advisable to
retain (or insert in brackets) the writer's own technical

terms, as there may not be an exact equivalent by which to render them. When the language is one's mother tongue, such a summary may simplify the author's statement, so that one can see more clearly what his position is, what evidence he brings forward, what arguments he uses. Such a summary may be a prelude to accepting his views, or it may be the first step to framing the criticisms on which they may be rejected. For the purely utilitarian purposes of an examination, the notes may provide a rapid means of revision. First the notes are read through carefully, perhaps with occasional reference to the book itself where a point is not sufficiently clear. Next they are looked through more rapidly at suitable intervals of time to provide the amount of over-learning necessary for retention. Finally, in order to clinch the matter, the successive headings may be memorized, so that any one of them may be paraded at need, bringing with it its subordinate train of sub-heads, arguments, facts, illustrations or criticisms.

To serve these purposes notes should emphasise the structure of the book from which they are made. Sometimes the writer himself supplies such a skeleton in the form of a table of contents or *table analytique*. This may indicate the matter of each chapter in a few headings, or it may supply a short summary, possibly, in either case, with page or paragraph references. Sometimes such a summary may be placed at the beginning of each chapter, sometimes it may be printed as a marginal rubric throughout. It may serve two purposes. To the reader approaching the work for the first time, it gives a bird's-eye view of the whole, if he is sufficiently familiar with the terms of the subject. To a less well equipped reader, it may afford at intervals a glimpse, as from a hill-top, of the country just ahead. Its second purpose is to help the reader who returns to the book, or who wishes to consult it on some special point, to find what he wants.

Even when such an analysis is supplied, the student may find it worth while to make his own, first, because it will be more closely adapted to his particular needs and purposes, and, secondly, because the attempt forces him to make up his own mind on each point as it arises. An attempt to express something in one's own words is the best way of finding out whether or not it has really been grasped.

The method to be adopted must vary with the subject matter and the author's treatment. If the matter is clearly and logically set out, the work is likely to be easy. If the statement is unnecessarily confused or involved, the task will be more difficult, but there will be the more reason to perform it. In the first case, if the book is the student's own, the simplest, and in some ways the most satisfactory plan is to mark the book itself with a pencil. This should not be a matter of conscience. There are some books which it would be sinful to mark—old books, rare books, books beautifully printed or produced, books to which a sentimental value attaches. There are other books which are to be regarded as tools to be used as best serves one's purpose, and, if the book is used up in the process, it is neither spoiled nor wasted, but has made a proper return for its owner's outlay. If its value to someone else is decreased, its value for its owner may be substantially increased. One may in a moment find what one wants in a marked copy of a book, and be at a loss with another copy even of the same edition. When the text of a book is to be submitted to intensive study, a copy interleaved with blank pages may be the most convenient means.

Little purpose is served by marking a book at random. It should be done on a plan related to the purpose for which the book is being read. If the intention is to master the book, then marking should aim at making clear the structure of the argument. If the intention is to criticise the book, it is necessary to distinguish points with which one is in agreement, and evidence or arguments which one can accept, from positions which one rejects and arguments or evidence which seem questionable. If the book is being read in relation to some purpose of the reader's rather than the author's, the emphasis may be entirely different from that of the author's summary, for what is incidental or subordinate from the author's point of view may be of primary importance for the reader.

The simplest case is that in which the book is to be mastered as a whole. Since the aim in marking is to draw attention to what is significant, it is first necessary to get some idea of the book as a whole. This may be done by studying the table of contents or the preface, if these are helpful, by reading, in the case of an established classic, some account of it in an encyclopædia or a history of the subject, or by glancing rapidly through the book itself in order to see what each chapter is about. The next step may be to go steadily through the book. There are two main things to look for—definitions of terms and statements of principles. Definitions may be indicated by underlining the term defined, and by some distinctive mark in the margin. Principles—that is, positions stated for defence or attack, theories suggested, hypotheses, conclusions—should be underlined and suitably indicated. Books vary in the degree to which their logical structure is made plain by the author. In some cases it is almost as clear as in geometry, where the successive principles (propositions, theorems) are separately enunciated, numbered, and even distinguished by special type, and then followed by a supporting

argument (proof), with the citation of the previously
established principles upon which it depends. In other
cases the logical skeleton, though equally complete,
may be so covered and concealed by literary artifice,
that close study may be needed to make it out. It is a
matter of fashion. The medieval thinker displayed his
logical processes openly. The modern writer usually
covers them up. Sometimes he shows discretion in
doing so.

The statement of a principle may be followed by
arguments or evidence in support of it, criticisms directed
against it by the writer or by his opponents, and answers
to these criticisms in turn. Marks should be used which
distinguish these and indicate their subordinate position.
One method is to number them in the margin. Sometimes a writer will himself distinguish them with " first,"
" secondly," etc. Sometimes he will merely say that he
will adduce so many points in evidence, and leave it to
the reader to distinguish them. Sometimes the evidence
or arguments come first, and the general statement comes
at the end of the paragraph or the chapter. In such
cases it is as well to look ahead for it, in order to know
where you are going.

As the student reads, he is now able to refer back to
definitions and principles, when there is need. He may
also see the importance of some statement which did not
sufficiently attract his attention when he first saw it,
and the path he has blazed through the earlier pages
will help him to find it. He should refer back freely as
he reads. In doing so he is knitting the different parts
of the book together in his mind, and building a systematic structure of memories instead of a linear chain.

When the structure of a book is not logical but
chronological, a different system is required. In a piece of
historical narrative we are introduced, not to a succession

of technical terms, but to a succession of persons, institutions or corporations, sometimes to so many that confusion easily results. It is a good plan to underline each such name at its first appearance, or rather at the point at which information is given about it. It is then easy to refer back as occasion requires. If the book has a good index, this may be done by referring to the index instead of by underlining, and when a doubt arises as to who or what Lord X or Mr. Y was, or where he came from, or what he was aiming at, a glance at each of the references to him will quickly give as complete a picture as that book can afford. It may be equally useful to read ahead in this way, by using the index. To look at the end of a novel to see what happens, may be weak-minded. We do not read history or biography for the mental tension of unsatisfied curiosity, but in order to understand some complex and many-sided transaction.

When the structure of a book is chronological, it is necessary to develop in one's mind a time scheme. The outstanding dates should be noted before beginning to read. Thus in the case of a biography you want first the dates of the birth and death of its subject. If the book is your own, it is a good plan to note them on the title page, if they are not there already. Every date, as it comes in, is then automatically referred to these as points of reference, and the subject's age at the time inferred. As one does this systematically the temporal relations of the events narrated gradually become clear. Some writers date successive events systematically, either in the text or in a rubric. Some scatter their dates rather casually, and leave it to the reader to infer from such phrases as " in the autumn of the following year " or " six years after his marriage," the date of which may in turn have to be inferred from " two years before accepting this appointment, he had married. . . . ."

In such a case it may be a good plan to make one's own rubric by reckoning the dates and entering them in the margin. Sometimes a complete table of dates is supplied at the beginning or at the end of the book, and it may be well to read with a bookmark at this point.

Narrative may be concerned with parallel series of events and these may be given seperate treatment. Thus four successive chapters may deal with the political, military, diplomatic and commercial history of the same period. This separation is for convenience only. These are four aspects of one story and it is necessary to bring them into one focus by setting them side by side, either mentally or on paper. A history of literature usually consists of little biographies, each giving the writer's works in chronological order. It may be just as important to note the relative dates of two works by different authors, as those of two works by the same author.

History, when it is more than a chronicle, is explanatory as well as narrative, though its terms of explanation follow a time sequence, one set of events giving rise to another. In so far as this is the case, it is a logical study, to be attacked by methods already described.

When the book may not be marked, we require a record of our reading. The simplest of all plans is to use a slip of paper as a bookmarker and note upon it the page on which any passage to which you want to refer again will be found. To do this it is only necessary to have a pencil in your pocket, and another at your bedside, if part of your reading is done in bed. These passages can then be reconsidered and copied later. Another plan is to copy the phrases or sentences which you would underline if the book were your own, but it may be necessary to do a little more than this, since the book itself will not be at hand if you want at some future time a little more information under these headings. It may therefore be necessary to make an abstract of important passages. Very often a word or a phrase will be enough to remind you of a particular argument or illustration. The page or chapter to which each note refers should of course be recorded. The first sheet should be headed with the author's name, the title of the book, and the place and date of publication. A shorter indication of the source of the note should head each sheet, since the sheets may become separated.

It is usually impossible to own all the books that one wants. Books have become steadily cheaper, but not correspondingly less in bulk, and an accumulation of books implies a more or less settled life. What books to possess is a matter which must vary with individual tastes and needs. Samuel Butler declared that he kept his books " at the British Museum and at Mudie's " and that " Webster's Dictionary, Whitaker's Almanack, and Bradshaw's Railway Guide should be sufficient for any ordinary library." Nowadays we can keep most of our books at our city or county libraries, particularly those which are expensive, and those not likely to be wanted frequently or at short notice. A book first read in this way may be bought later on. Unfortunately a library book usually has to be returned within a limited time, and so we cannot rely on the library for books for prolonged study.

Making notes of a lecture involves the same principles as making notes from a book. We want definitions, principles, an indication of the logical structure of the lecture, and a few words or phrases to remind us of illustrations, examples, quotations and references. There is one difficulty that does not occur in making notes from a book—we must listen, select and write, all at the same time ; and this puts a greater strain on the powers of attention. On the other hand, the lecturer may do more for us than the book, dictating an important sentence, building up his own summary on the blackboard, or summarising his argument as he goes along. The greatest mistake is to try to take down the lecture verbatim. The first aim should be to follow the lecture, so as to grasp its meaning ; the second to note its general course. Notes of a lecture that has not been understood in the course of listening to it are unlikely to be of any service. It is a good habit to look through lecture-notes at the earliest opportunity, correcting and amplifying where necessary, and calling to mind the matter of the lecture in greater detail than it was recorded. If this is done while the lecture is still fresh in the mind, it fulfils in relation to such material the two functions of recitation and over-learning.

Every human being is unique. There is no one else exactly like him. We recognise this in the case of our bodies and expect the tailor or the boot-maker to take some trouble to fit us with their wares. We differ still more in our mental make-up. This is not so evident, but a good teacher will study his pupil's ability, knowledge and skill, so that he may present each new lesson to him in the most suitable way. We cannot have books specially written for us, and so we must make the best of books which are more or less misfits—books which tell us many things that we know already, and many things that we do not want to know ; which fail to tell us the things we want or need ; which do not sufficiently explain what is new or difficult ; or which present their matter in an order which seemed a good one to the writer, but does not happen to suit us.

When the order of presentation adopted by a writer does not suit a particular reader, he may find a book heavy going, when he tries to plod conscientiously through it, and yet, when he opens it at random, he may come upon a passage which at once excites his interest, so that he reads on with pleasure. What should he do ? There can be only one answer—read on, as far as interest will carry him, and then look for some other passage which he can follow with equal satisfaction. In each case he is getting a foothold in the book. The passages which excite his interest are those which he can best understand, and interest and understanding mark the growing points of the mind. Interest and understanding may spread out from these points, till they cover the greater part of the book, leaving islands, instead of continents of unread matter. These islands are then less formidable in appearance, and more easily tackled because of what has been learned from the rest of the book. This method is not possible with all books, for in some cases what comes later cannot be understood, until what precedes it has been mastered. It should always be remembered that the purpose in reading a book is less that the book should be mastered than that the reader should be enlightened, that he should find in the book something that can be built up into the fabric of his own mind.

What we do not want, we can skip. What we do not understand, we must seek an explanation of elsewhere. A comparatively advanced work may assume in the reader knowledge which must be sought in a text-book of a more elementary character. A text-book is usually a rather concise summary of a branch of science or scholarship written with some examination in view. Its faults and its virtues derive from this fact. It is likely to be reliable, comprehensive and precise. It is also likely to be dull. If it has a good index it may make a good work of reference. It is often a good plan to go conscientiously through one text-book, while keeping an eye on one or two others on the same subject to supplement it where it is obscure, or for topics which it passes over.

Writing is reading in reverse. The writer's ideas must be put into words, so that they may be communicated to a reader. What one is to say and how one is to say it are in part determined by one's knowledge of the intended reader. Part of the difficulty of writing formal exercises comes from the fact that there is no real reader to write for. Matters are not much better when the prospective reader is an examiner. The reason is the same in both cases—there is no real process of communication.

There are two stages in writing—knowing what you want to say, and finding words to say it in. Sometimes they are not sharply divided. To sit down to write a friendly letter may be to have ideas and words come to mind together. In other cases material may be gathered, considered and reconsidered, arranged and rearranged, before pen is put to paper. The work is then in the condition of the book of which its author declared in reply to polite inquiries : " It is finished. There is nothing left to do but to write it ! "

If this method is followed, a piece of writing passes through a stage which corresponds closely to the notes or summaries made by a student in the course of his reading. The writer's thinking and planning are expressed in a summary, which sets out the structure of what he is to write—headings, sub-headings, and their subordinate arguments, examples, illustrations and instances.

In other cases the process of composition may seem to be almost the opposite of this. The writer's thoughts are put upon the paper without such elaborate preparation, and the plan becomes evident to the writer only when the writing is complete. In this sense Graham Wallas says in one of his prefaces :

> Now that the book is finished, I can see, . . . what it is about.*

It is a good thing to have a plan before beginning to write, but this plan may be modified and developed, or even abandoned, as the process of writing goes on. The shaping and ordering of the material is not all done by fully conscious mental processes, and what seems a difficulty, when considered in advance, may disappear, if the writer puts it aside and proceeds with the part of his job that he sees more clearly how to deal with. Ideas and words to express them do not always present themselves in the order in which they are sought. They should be noted when they occur. Such notes will be invaluable when the stage is reached when they may be incorporated, and it is worth a little trouble to record them. No doubt Milton's daughters thought it a bother, when called out of bed to take dictation, but *Paradise Lost* is the richer for the preservation of the inspirations which visited him in the night.

When we read, words are the medium through which we apprehend someone else's thoughts ; when we write, they are the means through which we express our own. Our acquaintance with a new word has two stages— that at which we recognise it and apprehend its meaning, and that at which we can use it to express what we want to say. Thus words which we understand easily, when we meet them in print, are not always readily, or safely, available, when we speak or write : and so our reading vocabularies are greater than our writing vocabularies. It is well to recognise this in learning a foreign language, and to be chary of using a word, until we have become

---

* *The Great Society.*

properly intimate with it by meeting it a number of times and in a number of different connections. The best preparation for speech or writing is ample experience of listening or reading.

The mechanical process of putting words upon paper has a greater importance than is sometimes supposed. The more attention has to be given to the pen or the typewriter, the less attention is available for the consideration of content and expression. Thus ease in writing is increased as the mechanical part of it becomes more automatic. Writing has two aspects of importance—speed and legibility. The best writing is that which can be produced most easily and quickly, provided it can be easily read. Speed is easily measured. The usual method is to ask the subject to write the line *Mary had a little lamb* as many times as he can in 30 seconds, giving him the signal to start and to stop. The number of letters written, multiplied by two, is then the writer's speed in letters per minute. One hundred and twenty-two of the writer's graduate students had writing speeds, measured in this way, which varied between 45 and 115 letters per minute.

The fast writers would seem to have a real advantage in making notes from a book or taking lecture notes. In these cases legibility is also important ; notes which are hard to decipher are less likely to be carefully studied, or involve extra time and labour in copying out.

A fast writer does not necessarily produce a less legible script than slow writers. Greater speed results from greater skill and the use of simple and distinctive letter forms. Fatigue may be greatly reduced by adopting a suitable posture in which the writing movements are freely and easily made. Some economy in time and fatigue may be achieved in making notes for one's own use by the adoption of abbreviations for recurrent terms or phrases.

Figuring differs from writing in that each figure must be separately legible, whereas, in writing, individual letters may merge into the form of the word as a whole without loss of legibility. It is therefore well to adopt for figuring forms which are simple and not liable to be confused with one another when hastily made, and to avoid varying them. A considerable increase in accuracy in computation may result from neater figuring and a little care in alignment.

To have regular periods of the day or of the week for rest or recreation is just as important as to have regular periods for work. Physical exercise is of first importance, preferably in the open air. In this matter needs and tastes differ, and each must decide for himself what kind and what amount of exercise is necessary for the bodily health which is an essential condition of mental fitness. Scholars have gone to absurd and unprofitable extremes in this matter. Lytton relates of a character in one of his novels that he looked back upon only one ill-spent day in his life, the day of his wedding, when he got no more than eight hours for reading. Such concentration upon passive absorption may produce not the scholar but :

> The bookful blockhead, ignorantly read,
> With loads of learned lumber in his head,* . . .

Mere reading unilluminated by experience and reflection is of little value, and this no doubt is what Hobbes meant, when he said (as reported by Aubrey) that " if he had read as much as other men, he should have known no more than other men." The younger Pliny† says of his uncle :

> . . . his whole time was devoted to study without intermission, excepting only when he bathed. In this

---

* A. Pope—*An Essay on Criticism*, ll, 612-3. Everyman's Library.
† *Letters*, III, 5. Tr. W. Melmoth.

exception I include no more than the time he was actually in the bath ; for while he was rubbed and wiped, he was employed either in hearing some book read to him or in dictating . . . he once reproved me for walking : " You might," said he, " employ those hours to more advantage " : for he thought every hour lost, that was not given to study.

This would not be for most of us a profitable mental regime.

The problem of periods of work, and rest or recreation, has been studied experimentally. Work produces fatigue in the sense of lessened efficiency at the work. Rest or recreation removes the fatigue. The most effective form of rest is sleep and an adequate number of hours of refreshing sleep in the course of every twenty-four is a necessary condition of bodily health and mental vigour. Actual bodily disorders may result from insufficient sleep. The optimum number of hours varies from person to person, and with age. It is greatest in childhood, smallest in old age. Few can with advantage limit themselves to the four or five hours that sufficed for Napoleon or Edison. An hour stolen from the night is not an hour gained, if each hour of the following day gives only sixty or seventy per cent. of the advantage that it otherwise would. Hours of sleep should be regular. The effects of one late night may not be entirely effaced in a week of normal hours.

The level of efficiency varies during any period of work. Apart from casual variations, there are two of a regular kind. There is at the beginning a period of " warming up," of adapting ourselves to the task in hand. It corresponds to the first few balls at cricket, during which a batsman " plays himself in," taking no risks till he is sure that eye, motor centres, nerves and muscles are all ready to play their parts. The student may find a real difficulty in settling down to a period of useful study. It may save valuable time, if he makes a practice of leaving books and papers so arranged at the end of one spell of work that it is easy to pick up the threads again. It is also useful to choose a stopping point—one at which there is some interest excited which will bring him back to his desk with some eagerness. On the other hand to persist until interest is exhausted or until fatigue and discouragement compel you to break off, is to put an unnecessary difficulty in the way of a re-start. It may be useful to make it a matter of routine to begin a period of work with some task which does not call at once for one's maximum effort. Trollope relates in his autobiography that it was his practice to be at his table every morning at 5.30 a.m., and to work for three hours, during which he habitually wrote some 2,500 words.

> . . . my three hours were not devoted entirely to writing. I always began my task by reading through the work of the day before, an operation which would take me half an hour, . . . by reading what he has last written, just before he recommences his task, the writer will catch the spirit of what he is then saying.*

An excellent example of " warming-up."

The second variation in efficiency is due to the onset of fatigue. As we continue any mental or muscular activity, it requires greater effort, less is accomplished in a given time, and we make more mistakes. This lessened efficiency leads at last to a point at which it is unprofitable to continue longer, or even to a point at which it is impossible to do so, even at the prompting of the most powerful motive.

Investigation shows that fatigue is not all of one kind

---

* A. Trollope—*An Autobiography*, Chapt. XV.

Muscular fatigue appears to be purely physical. The continued movement of a muscle produces chemical substances, which so affect the structure through which nervous energy passes from the motor nerve to the muscle cells, that it can no longer do so. This kind of fatigue is studied experimentally by means of the *ergograph*, a piece of apparatus in which a weight, attached to a cord passing over a pulley, is raised and lowered by the flexing and extending of the subject's middle finger in time with a metronome. The distance through which it is raised steadily decreases as the muscle becomes fatigued, until at last successive efforts to bend the finger result in no visible movement of the weight. Thus a state of complete fatigue is reached in a period of a minute or two.

Mental fatigue does not lead to a similar result. In order to find the effects on efficiency of continued mental work, Dr. Arai, an American psychologist, worked for four days from 11 a.m. to 11 p.m. at a task requiring a very high degree of attention and effort. She multiplied in her head a series of pairs of four-figure numbers, such, for example, as 7,893 multiplied by 3,654. In each case she memorized the figures, multiplied them mentally, wrote down the answer, and proceeded to memorize the next set of figures. She found that at the end of each day the time taken to work an example was approximately doubled. Thus the loss in efficiency was small compared with that found in experiments with the ergograph, and there would seem to be comparatively little importance to be attached to purely mental fatigue. It should be remembered that multiplication is an activity based upon long established habits. These results therefore do not necessarily apply to mental activities of a different kind—for example, those involving processes of active or creative thought.

Dr. Arai declared that during the experiment her dominant desire was to obtain correct fatigue curves. If the reader will try such a series of mental multiplications, he will probably find that he will not work very many examples, if indeed he completes one, before his interest in the attempt disappears, and he gives up and turns to something else. Thus one factor in work, which we readily mistake for fatigue, is boredom, due to the exhaustion of interest in the task, and the competition of other interests.

The fatigue produced by study is a combination of all these three factors. There is actual bodily fatigue—muscular fatigue due to the continuation in one posture, to the movements of writing, typing, holding a book, fatigue of the muscles of the eyes. There is probably some fatigue which may be described as mental, fatigue of the nerve centres involved in intellectual processes. There is certainly increasing difficulty in holding oneself to the task, and repressing competing interests and impulses—the impulse to get up and move about, to get into the fresh air, to relax the mental tension over something which makes a smaller demand upon the attention, to set about one's other business or amusements.

Fatigue has been shown to be an important factor in industry, so that it is advantageous, from the point of view of the worker's health and output, to limit hours of work, and to arrange them so as to produce the minimum of fatigue.* Factory work is largely repetitive, and movements which have been brought to a high pitch of efficiency by repetition are likely to be less affected by fatigue than those more recently acquired. It follows that the student, who is continually engaged in doing what he has not yet learned to do automatically, and in

---

* See for example, May Smith—*An Introduction to Industrial Psychology.*

thinking in ways which still require from him a special effort of attention, is likely to feel the effects of fatigue more quickly. He must therefore keep his mind and body at a high pitch of efficiency, and either work for shorter hours or vary the nature of his work at intervals.

This points to his special need for a healthy mode of life—a moderate diet, temperate habits, regular exercise and sleep, attention to bodily defects, particularly defects of teeth, digestion or eyes. Attention to these, and to the organisation of his work, may enable him to put in as many hours a day at his more exacting tasks, as others do at repetitive work.

Harm to mind or body is not likely to result from too much study. It may however result from ill-regulated hours of study and insufficient exercise or recreation. Overstrain may result from excessively large and indigestible meals—cramming in a short time material that should be assimilated more slowly. There is no time to obtain a proper mastery over it, and so what has been passed over too quickly does not illuminate what follows it. Overstrain is a normal consequence of attempting tasks beyond one's mental powers. Contrary to popular beliefs, it is not the intelligent child at school that suffers in this way, but the not so intelligent child, trying to keep up with the more intelligent, who is carrying his load easily. The student may produce a similar result by tackling in an ineffective way tasks which would be well within his powers, if he gave himself a better chance.

INDEX

NOTE

Some readers have vainly sought the word referred to in the Note on p. 205. It will be found, with both spellings, on pp. 158–9. It occurs most frequently in Chapter X. Both spellings are scattered through the book, but, as they are both admissible, they do not attract attention.